Nowinski and Baker have thorough̲ly ̲̲̲̲̲̲̲̲ ̲̲̲̲̲̲̲ ̲̲̲̲̲̲̲ ̲ ̲ ̲ume, resulting in an essential book for anyone working with addicted individuals. This is a comprehensive guide to implementing Twelve Step oriented psychotherapy, including both theoretical understanding and practical applications. This book stands as a powerful rejoinder to those who ignore or minimize the relevance of Twelve Step programs in supporting recovery. Nowinski and Baker have done themselves proud, and have done the field a lasting service.

—Mark Schenker, PhD,
Author of *A Clinician's Guide to 12-Step Recovery*

With this book, the authors have created an important contribution to our understanding of the Twelve Steps and the value of the Twelve Step Facilitation program. . . . They explain how Twelve Step Facilitation (TSF) bolsters the principles behind the Twelve Steps by incorporating them into a professionally-driven treatment program, thereby increasing their efficacy. This book is an extremely valuable resource for clinicians, researchers, and educators, as well as for others who are interested in the Twelve Step program and its application to professional treatment.

—Dr. Richard Juman,
Editor, Pro Voices, TheFix.com

The latest version of *Twelve Step Facilitation Handbook* proves to be an invaluable resource for helping professionals. It provides the critical addition of [TSF] Elective Topic 5: Spirituality, which cuts to the core of addiction treatment. Summary tables capture key concepts and processes, and the authors provide clear explanations of the ways in which TSF supports individualized care across the treatment and recovery spectrum.

An essential tool in the toolbox for anyone who embraces the Twelve Steps as an adjunct to treatment, it stands as a compelling read for gaining a better understanding of not only how TSF functions, but also how its rich tradition is woven into the fabric of modern day evidence-based practice.

—Cara Renzelli, PhD,
Vice President, Operations and
Clinical Advancement, Gateway Rehab

Twelve Step Facilitation Handbook

A Therapeutic Approach to Treatment and Recovery

Second Edition

Joseph Nowinski, PhD, and Stuart Baker

Hazelden
Publishing

Hazelden Publishing
Center City, Minnesota 55012
hazelden.org/bookstore

Originally published by Lexington Books 1992. Originally titled *The Twelve-Step Facilitation Handbook: A Systematic Approach to Early Recovery from Alcoholism and Addiction*. First published by Hazelden Foundation as *The Twelve-Step Facilitation Handbook: A Systematic Approach to Recovery from Substance Dependence*.

Published by Jossey-Bass, Inc., Publishers 1998
First published by Hazelden Foundation 2003
Second edition published by Hazelden Publishing 2017
Printed in the United States of America

Library of Congress Cataloging-in-Publication Data

Names: Nowinski, Joseph, author. | Baker, Stuart, 1951– author.
Title: Twelve step facilitation handbook : a therapeutic approach to
    treatment and recovery / Joseph Nowinski, PhD, and Stuart Baker.
Description: Second edition. | Center City, Minnesota : Hazelden Publishing,
    2017. | Includes bibliographical references and index.
Identifiers: LCCN 2017023588 | ISBN 9781616497668 (softcover)
Subjects: LCSH: Twelve-step programs. | Drug addicts—Rehabilitation. |
    Alcoholics—Rehabilitation.
Classification: LCC RC564 .N69 2017 | DDC 616.86/06—dc23
LC record available at https://lccn.loc.gov/2017023588

Editor's note
The names, details, and circumstances may have been changed to protect the privacy of those mentioned in this publication.

This publication is not intended as a substitute for the advice of health care professionals.

Readers should be aware that websites listed in this work may have changed or disappeared between when this work was written and when it is read.

Alcoholics Anonymous, AA, and the Big Book are registered trademarks of Alcoholics Anonymous World Services, Inc. Hazelden Publishing offers a variety of information on addiction and related areas. The views and interpretations expressed herein are those of the authors and are neither endorsed nor approved by AA or any Twelve Step organization.

21 20   3 4 5 6

Cover design: Terri Kinne
Interior design: Terri Kinne
Typesetting: Percolator Graphic Design

For Maggie, Rebecca, and Gregory with love, from J. N.

and

for Mar-c, Aaron, and Maya: thank you for your
inspiration and support, from S. B.

CONTENTS

PART 1

Principles of
Twelve Step Facilitation

Introduction

Alcoholics Anonymous (AA) and other Twelve Step fellowships are programs of hope and renewal that were born of despair and personal destruction. The origin of AA can be traced to two individuals—a stockbroker in New York City and a physician in Akron, Ohio, who made the seminal discovery that two alcoholics could increase their chances of staying sober if they met often, talked honestly, and supported each other's sobriety. That discovery has remained at the core of Alcoholics Anonymous (as well as other recovery fellowships) since 1935. Proof that AA has emerged as an integral part of successful recovery for people throughout the world can be seen in the growth this voluntary, self-supporting fellowship has experienced.

A Brief History of Alcoholics Anonymous

At its most elemental level, AA can be understood as a method for helping those who no longer wish to drink (or use drugs) to stay sober, one day at a time. It is a program that relies on the principle of attraction rather than promotion, meaning it welcomes those who seek out the program's support rather than promote the program to those who may not wish to participate or who would deal with their drinking through some other means. AA was—and at heart still is—a program for those who want it: for those men and women who believe that they've tried everything they care to try to moderate their drinking (or drug use), and who now have a desire to stop altogether.

The founders of AA were influenced early on by the likes of the psychoanalyst Carl Jung and the philanthropist John D. Rockefeller. The former offered the opinion that the only hope for someone with a severe alcohol use disorder was some form of spiritual transformation, while the latter declined to support AA financially, arguing that it would be better off being self-supporting and beholden to no one (see www.aa.org, "Archives & History"). Those ideas in turn found their way into the Twelve Step program of AA and its traditions of being voluntary, spiritually oriented, and self-supporting.

Bill W. and Dr. Bob S., cofounders of AA, were also influenced by their experiences with the Oxford Group movement—a spiritually based organization whose goal was self-improvement. Oxford Group members believed that this could best be achieved by pursuing the following:

- ongoing self-monitoring or maintaining an ongoing awareness of one's personal flaws and shortcomings
- public admission of one's flaws and shortcomings in the context of Oxford Group meetings
- making personal amends as appropriate to those harmed as a consequence of one's flaws or shortcomings

These Oxford Group tenets found their way into the Twelve Step program that became the basis of AA.

Today, AA remains true to its fundamental traditions, which include

- **Anonymity**—This tradition serves two purposes. First, it protects the privacy of AA members. Equally important, the tradition of anonymity serves as a barrier to anyone who might seek personal gain, power, or self-aggrandizement through the fellowship.
- **Attraction, not promotion**—AA and its sister fellowships do not advertise, nor do they evangelize or enter the community to convert others to their beliefs. Rather, they remain free and open to anyone who voluntarily chooses to enter a meeting. In this same vein, AA by tradition eschews public controversy. It has no spokesperson, no public relations office.
- **Self-support**—Early on, Bill W. was approached by Dr. Charles Towns, owner of Towns Hospital in New York City, who proposed that Bill treat people with alcohol use disorders in his hospital according to the Twelve Step program and that they share in the revenue generated by that treatment. Bill W. opted to follow

Rockefeller's advice, and AA has remained self-supporting through the voluntary contributions of its members ever since. There is also a cap on individual yearly contributions.

- **Spirituality and pragmatism**—Two parallel strains dominate the AA culture. On the one hand, there are the social/behavioral traditions: attend meetings, get a sponsor and a home group, and so on. But there is also a parallel tradition that seeks to promote spiritual practices (self-inventory, making amends, being rigorously honest, prayer and meditation) aimed at promoting a "spiritual awakening."

Alcoholics Anonymous and Professional Treatment

It is of interest that AA by tradition does not affiliate with or endorse any professional treatment programs (including the one presented here). What that means is that there are no standards by which to measure any claims that treatment centers adhere to the AA model of recovery. This allows for a great deal of diversity in the actual content of such programs. The first recorded attempt to integrate the Twelve Steps of AA into actual treatment took place in the 1950s at Willmar State Hospital in Minnesota by a psychologist, Daniel J. Anderson, and a psychiatrist, Nelson Bradley. According to Anderson's first-person account, "The key element of this novel approach to addiction treatment was the blending of professional and trained nonprofessional (recovering) staff around the principles of Alcoholics Anonymous (AA)."[1] Later, this "Minnesota Model" of treatment was instituted at the Hazelden Foundation, a nonprofit treatment center based in Minnesota, now called the Hazelden Betty Ford Foundation. From there, the model proliferated alongside the growth of AA itself.

The Twelve Steps of Alcoholics Anonymous[2]

1. We admitted we were powerless over alcohol—that our lives had become unmanageable.

2. Came to believe that a Power greater than ourselves could restore us to sanity.

3. Made a decision to turn our will and our lives over to the care of God *as we understood Him.*

4. Made a searching and fearless moral inventory of ourselves.

5. Admitted to God, to ourselves, and to another human being the exact nature of our wrongs.

6. Were entirely ready to have God remove all these defects of character.

7. Humbly asked Him to remove our shortcomings.

8. Made a list of all persons we had harmed, and became willing to make amends to them all.

9. Made direct amends to such people wherever possible, except when to do so would injure them or others.

10. Continued to take personal inventory and when we were wrong promptly admitted it.

11. Sought through prayer and meditation to improve our conscious contact with God *as we understood Him,* praying only for knowledge of His will for us and the power to carry that out.

12. Having had a spiritual awakening as the result of these steps, we tried to carry this message to alcoholics, and to practice these principles in all our affairs.

Research on Alcoholics Anonymous and the Twelve Step Model of Recovery

Because of its traditions, AA has never engaged in formal research regarding the effectiveness of its Twelve Step program in relation to recovery. The closest it comes is its triennial member surveys, which ask a voluntary sample of members to share their age and sex, how many meetings they attend, whether they have a sponsor and a home group, how long they have been sober, and so on. The survey results have been published by AA every three years since 1977, and they have proven to be quite robust and consistent. That said, the surveys are not controlled clinical research. Moreover, since AA avoids public controversy, others are free to criticize its surveys and assert that Twelve Step programs are ineffective (or even harmful)—all with no rejoinder from AA.

Prior to 1989 there was a notable dearth of scientific research on the

AA approach to be found in professional literature—despite the fact that so many treatment programs claimed to endorse it. That led the prestigious Institute of Medicine (IOM) to issue a white paper in 1989 with the following conclusion: "Alcoholics Anonymous, one of the most widely used approaches to recovery in the United States, remains one of the least rigorously evaluated."[3]

The IOM white paper in turn led to more than two decades of rigorous research on AA and the effectiveness of the Twelve Step model. A group of renowned professionals in the field summarized their review of the research as follows: "Because longitudinal studies associate self-help group involvement with reduced substance use, improved psychosocial functioning, and lessened health care costs, there are humane and practical reasons to develop self-help group supportive policies."[4]

Twelve Step Facilitation (TSF), the subject of this book, is an evidence-based treatment program rooted in research on Twelve Step recovery. Some of that research will be reviewed in greater depth, as it is relevant to the implementation of specific TSF topics. Peer review of this body of research led to TSF being included in the National Registry of Evidence-based Programs and Practices (www.nrepp.samhsa.gov). It has been recognized as an effective approach for the treatment of substance use disorders (alcohol and other drugs), even when compared to alternative treatments (comparative evaluation research). It can be implemented both individually and in a group format.

Project MATCH

The Institute of Medicine's white paper served as the impetus for much rigorous research on the Twelve Step model of recovery. The largest psychotherapy outcome study conducted to date is Project MATCH (Matching Alcoholism Treatments to Client Heterogeneity). MATCH was intended to compare three conceptually different approaches to treating alcohol use disorders. These treatments were

- Cognitive-behavioral therapy (CBT): The main goal of CBT is to change thinking in order to change behaviors. Using a CBT approach to a substance use disorder involves assuming that substance use represents a dysfunctional means of coping, such as with stress. CBT focuses on teaching participants healthy coping skills. It can help participants identify risky situations, resist use in risky situations, and so on.

- Motivational enhancement therapy (MET): MET assumes that men and women can and will find their own solutions for a substance use disorder, *once they decide they have one.* An MET approach uses internal motivation for change, such as pointing out negative consequences that have been associated with past and ongoing substance use.

- Twelve Step Facilitation (TSF): The goal of TSF is to facilitate active involvement in a fellowship of peers that supports abstinence from substance use. Abstinence is supported through fellowship, bibliotherapy such as conference-approved and/or facilitator-recommended literature, and adherence to the principles of the Twelve Steps and Twelve Traditions of Alcoholics Anonymous and other Twelve Step fellowships.

The title of the study, Project MATCH, describes the two inherent goals. The first goal was to assess just how effective each of the three treatment approaches were, and the second goal was to find indicators in patients that would match them to the best treatment program. Program success was based on outcome measures that included total abstinence from alcohol use; percent days abstinent (PDA)—a measure of how many days a subject drank in terms of a percentage; and drinks per drinking day (DDD)—how many drinks a subject consumed when he or she did drink. Researchers were interested in measuring abstinence and progression toward abstinence.

The second goal of Project MATCH focused on finding out whether a particular treatment modality might be more effective with a certain type of patient. For example, one hypothesis was that TSF would prove to be more effective for those subjects with the most severe alcohol use disorders—in other words, those who had "bottomed out." Similarly, it was predicted that TSF would be more effective for men than women, largely because Alcoholics Anonymous was initially founded by men.

The Project MATCH study spanned seven years and included nine treatment sites across the United States. Five were outpatient sites, which recruited subjects from the local community. Four were aftercare sites that accepted subjects as they exited inpatient treatment. The data it collected led to numerous publications. We'll focus on the one-year and three-year post-treatment outcomes.[5]

All three treatment modalities (CBT, MET, and TSF) proved effective at reducing alcohol use (PDA and DDD). These findings were surprising to some, for it was common at the time for professionals to be skeptical about the effectiveness of any treatment for an alcohol use disorder. But perhaps the bigger surprise was in finding that TSF was sometimes superior to both CBT and MET. The principal developer of MET, Dr. William Miller, expressed it this way:

> On at least one time-honored outcome measure—the percentage of patients maintaining complete abstinence—those in the Twelve-Step Facilitation treatment fared significantly better at all follow-up points than did patients in the other two conditions—a substantial advantage of about 10 percentage points that endured across 3 years.[6]

Project MATCH data clearly show that one year after treatment, men and women randomly assigned to TSF had more than double the number of continuously abstinent individuals than those assigned to CBT or MET. Additionally, those individuals were 33 percent more likely to remain continually abstinent *three years* after treatment.

Subsequent randomized clinical trials conducted by other researchers have replicated and confirmed the Project MATCH findings,[7] and in 2014 two Harvard Medical School faculty members publicly defended TSF against criticism by reiterating the efficacy seen in Project MATCH data and clarifying incorrect interpretations.[8] Studies have shown that engagement in AA or another Twelve Step fellowship following treatment for a substance use disorder not only increases abstinence rates by about 33 percent but also decreases health care costs by 64 percent when compared to CBT.[9]

Despite the evidence, criticism of AA and the Twelve Step model persists. This may be because Twelve Step fellowships strictly adhere to being "programs of attraction," not promotion. In other words, Twelve Step fellowships welcome any individual who has "a desire to stop." AA, Marijuana Anonymous (MA), and Narcotics Anonymous (NA) have no public relations office, much less a spokesperson. Twelve Step world services offices do not respond to criticism, which can be unfounded and based on prejudice and misinformation. Twelve Step fellowships do not claim to be the only pathway to recovery. But *Alcoholics Anonymous,* the basic text for AA, states, "Rarely have we seen a person fail who has thoroughly followed our path."[10]

Target Audience for Twelve Step Facilitation

Research on the effectiveness of TSF naturally raises a clinical question: For whom is abstinence an appropriate treatment goal, thereby making TSF an appropriate treatment option? This question arises out of an even deeper question: Are there individuals whose substance use might be better treated through interventions aimed at moderation or harm reduction? Though there is no hard-and-fast rule, treatment is recommended for moderate to severe substance use disorders by the American Psychiatric Association (see chapter 6, pages 65–75).

Figure 1. Substance Use Spectrum

According to figure 1, substance use is measured along a spectrum that ranges from low-risk, infrequent use at one end to a severe substance use disorder on the other end. Mild problems may be amenable to interventions aimed at helping individuals return to low-risk use. The further right one moves on the spectrum, however, the more abstinence from substance use becomes the most reasonable goal to pursue. People who have a moderate substance use disorder are at the highest risk of developing a more severe problem. It is up to the person facilitating TSF, after a clinical interview that includes a diagnostic assessment, to determine where the participant falls on the spectrum and what goal is most appropriate.

■ ■ ■

Important Considerations

The purpose of this handbook is to educate professional counselors, facilitators, and trained peer counselors/coaches on the theory, supportive research, and practice of Twelve Step Facilitation (TSF), which can be thought of as "psychotherapy-assisted recovery." The concepts and principles that form the basis for TSF are described in detail here, as well as the structure and content of the program. TSF is a comprehensive therapy that addresses three dimensions of recovery: social/behavioral, cognitive, and spiritual. This handbook also describes the Twelve Step Facilitation for Co-occurring Disorders (TSF-COD) program, an adaptation of TSF for use with individuals who have co-occurring substance use and psychiatric disorders. Instructions for program implementation can be found in *Twelve Step Facilitation Facilitator Guide* and *Twelve Step Facilitation for Co-occurring Disorders Facilitator Guide*. Recommendations are provided throughout the program for group implementation of TSF.

Assessment

Many individuals who enter treatment for substance use disorders do so after a detailed biopsychosocial assessment. Assessment is a core topic in the TSF program and will be described in detail in chapter 6 on pages 65–75. A thorough assessment not only helps determine an accurate diagnosis for participants; it also helps create an individualized treatment plan. Many treatment centers follow their own protocols, but instruments that exhibit reliability and validity are usually included in a complete diagnostic assessment. A comprehensive mental health evaluation helps identify co-occurring disorders as well, another important step in developing an individualized treatment plan. Assessment at this stage will likely include the diagnostic criteria for substance use disorders found in the American Psychiatric Association's *Diagnostic and Statistical Manual of Mental Disorders, Fifth Edition (DSM-5)*, but other common resources for assessment include the Minnesota Multiphasic Personality Inventory (MMPI), the Personality Assessment Inventory (PAI), and the criteria set forth by the American Society of Addiction Medicine (ASAM criteria). Some tools test participants for both substance use disorders and other mental health concerns. For example, the Behavioral Health Index–Multimedia Version (BHI-MV)[1] includes the evidence-based Addiction Severity Index–Multimedia Version (ASI-MV) as well as an analysis of broader mental health issues. Each participant has his or her own unique set of diagnostic considerations, so thorough evaluation is very important for establishing a treatment plan.

Facilitator Guides

In addition to this handbook, two companion facilitator guides for program administration are available: *Twelve Step Facilitation Facilitator Guide* and *Twelve Step Facilitation for Co-occurring Disorders Facilitator Guide*. Whereas this handbook focuses more on the research, structure, and theory behind TSF, the facilitator guides provide session-by-session, step-by-step overviews of the program designed specifically for the facilitator. Each contains straightforward instruction on complete program administration. Included within each facilitator guide (and on the CD-ROM that accompanies the guide) are checklists for each topic, and the checklists can be used in two ways:

- *As guides for conducting specific sessions.* Facilitators can conveniently print and use the checklists during sessions. Initially developed for use in clinical trials, participants reported no trouble with facilitators referring to these checklists. In fact, participants generally like that the facilitator can structure the sessions around the achievement of specific goals. We therefore encourage facilitators to bring these checklists into actual TSF sessions and refer to them as needed.

- *As a means of measuring treatment fidelity.* Observers and clinical supervisors can utilize the session guidelines to monitor how strictly facilitators are adhering to the treatment protocol.

Target Population

As stated earlier, TSF is recommended for individuals who qualify for a diagnosis of a moderate to severe substance use disorder, according to *DSM-5* criteria (see page 65 in chapter 6). Accordingly, we recommend using reliable, valid diagnostic tools to help individuals accurately and honestly assess their reality and decide whether abstinence and the support of a peer fellowship is the best option for solving the problem. TSF can be used with both adult and adolescent populations, in either an individual or a group setting.

Flexibility

This program provides straightforward content with a flexible structure that enables facilitators to define specific goals and assess participants' ongoing progress in meeting those goals. Both TSF and TSF-COD can be used with individuals who have no prior exposure to Twelve Step fellowships, and also with those who have prior exposure through treatment or voluntary attendance of Alcoholics Anonymous (AA), Marijuana Anonymous (MA), Narcotics Anonymous (NA), or other mutual support meetings. Both TSF and TSF-COD include core and elective topics to allow for individualized treatment planning that addresses the unique concerns of each participant rather than offering a "one-size-fits-all" approach to treatment that less adequately addresses individual participant needs.

Recovery versus Cure

Twelve Step fellowships like AA, MA, and NA assume that there is no *cure* for alcoholism or other drug addiction. In speaking of *recovery* from addiction, they emphasize the concept of "arrest" as opposed to "cure." Effectively this means accepting the idea that one must forego alcohol and other drugs forever. As the book *Narcotics Anonymous* states, "We realize that we are never cured, and that we carry the disease within us for the rest of our lives. We have a disease, but we do recover." [2]

Regardless of whether one chooses to refer to addiction as a physical disease or a complex biopsychosocial-spiritual disorder, Twelve Step fellowships are based on the idea that recovery is an ongoing process that requires vigilance along with mutual support. Facilitation of TSF and TSF-COD are consequently intended to coincide with participants' active and ongoing involvement in Twelve Step fellowships (although any fellowship whose goal is to support abstinence from substance use is also appropriate). The correlation between fellowship involvement and recovery has been well established, and it impacts efficacy of the TSF and TSF-COD treatment programs. In other words, the role of fellowship in TSF and TSF-COD is directly related to treatment outcomes, so its importance cannot be overstated. Involvement in a fellowship beyond meeting attendance lends key support throughout the recovery process. For many, the additional support that occurs outside of meetings plays a significant role in continued sobriety—the welcoming nature of fellowship often includes grabbing coffee after meetings, eating meals with others who attend meetings, and exchanging phone numbers or email addresses for accessible support.

Twelve Step fellowships are based on the assumptions that severe substance use disorders

- are chronic conditions of complex etiology that progressively affect the body, mind, and spirit
- are characterized by a person's inability to reliably control his or her use of alcohol and/or other drugs
- have only one effective remedy—abstinence from the use of all mood-altering substances

The AA fellowship of peers that evolved from the early work of Bill W. and others is rooted in the idea that one's addiction (what is now referred to as a severe substance use disorder) can best be arrested by reaching out to fellow addicts. The Twelve Steps of AA are therefore not a treatment program but a suggested pathway for ongoing *recovery*. The essence of this recovery is a changed lifestyle (one's habits and social network) along with personal improvement or spiritual growth.

In the view of fellowships such as AA, MA, and NA, once a person is addicted, sustaining sobriety requires ongoing vigilance. The goal for someone recovering from a substance use disorder is to become actively involved in a program that will help him or her avoid taking the first drink or drug dose that will re-ignite his or her compulsion to drink or use without limit. Twelve Step fellowships provide the social vehicle for such vigilance, while the Twelve Steps represent a blueprint for personal renewal and for healing the personal and social wounds that result from substance use.

For the man or woman whose use meets the diagnostic criteria for a severe substance use disorder, the most appropriate goal is daily sobriety; hence, recovery is pursued "One day at a time," and the recovering individual is reinforced within the fellowship for each day of sobriety. So while longevity in sobriety is celebrated, recovery is experienced anew every day, and even the first day of sobriety following a slip is grounds for recognition.

The enemies of recovery include complacency, forgetfulness, and arrogance ("self-centeredness"). Relapse occurs well before the first drink is taken or the first drug is used. Relapse begins when ongoing, active recovery stops. It begins when the person with a substance use disorder feels "safe" enough to stop going to meetings, or "safe" enough to have a single drink (or take a single pill). It begins when he or she stops remembering the harm done (both to others and to himself or herself) as a consequence of his or her substance use disorder (for example, what it was like to lose a job, lose friends, ruin a relationship, damage his or her own health, or experience guilt, hopelessness, and self-hatred). It begins when the individual decides that group support is no longer needed.

Recovery can be considered a spiritual journey in that people in recovery from a substance use disorder need to change habits, values, and attitudes. As addiction progresses, values, priorities, relationships, and even goals tend to yield to the need to pursue the addiction. The individual regresses developmentally to a more and more juvenile, self-centered state. Conversely, as recovery progresses, isolation gives way to involvement, alienation gives way to friendship, and arrogance, defensiveness, and grandiosity give way to humility and gratitude. Most people in recovery (though not all) eventually come to believe in some power greater than themselves. For many, that power is identified as the fellowship itself; for others, it may be the value of prayer and/or meditation. In this way, the Twelve Steps are a guide to the spiritual journey that is an integral part of recovery.

The Twelve Step Path to Recovery

TSF and TSF-COD seek to facilitate participants' active participation in Twelve Step fellowships. "Working the program" is the primary factor responsible for sustained sobriety in both TSF and TSF-COD; accordingly, active involvement in fellowship groups is the primary desired outcome of the program. Research that sheds light on what constitutes this "active involvement" will be cited as we move ahead.

According to the views of fellowship groups such as AA, MA, and NA, addiction marks the end point of a chronic and progressive process that, if not arrested, may lead to insanity or death. Addiction is characterized by a loss of one's ability to control (limit) or stop one's use of one or more mood-altering substances. The book *Alcoholics Anonymous* states, "We alcoholics are men and women who have lost the ability to control our drinking. We know that no real alcoholic *ever* recovers control."[3]

The NA view of drug addiction parallels the AA view of alcoholism: "As addicts, we have an incurable disease called addiction. The disease is chronic, progressive and fatal."[4]

Progression of a substance use disorder, from mild to moderate to severe, has a predictable course and produces specific and predictable effects on individuals. In addition to its physical effects, addiction also affects its victims on cognitive, emotional, social, and spiritual levels. It is a story of a gradual but steady decline in overall functioning, to the point of "bottoming out."

> We reached a point in our lives where we felt like a lost cause. We had little worth to family, friends or on the job. Many of us were unemployed and unemployable. Any form of success was frightening and unfamiliar. We didn't know what to do. As the feeling of self-loathing grew, we needed to use more and more to mask our feelings. We were sick and tired of pain and trouble. We were frightened and ran from the fear. No matter how far we ran, we always carried fear with us. We were hopeless, useless and lost. Failure had become our way of life and self-esteem was non-existent. Perhaps the most painful feeling of all was the desperation.
>
> —*Narcotics Anonymous*[5]

Perhaps the most important tradition that is shared in fellowship meetings is the telling of personal stories of decline, followed by renewal. A common theme for all addiction stories is how it was, what happened, and how it is now. The purpose of this storytelling at meetings is not to boast about drunken exploits or to garner sympathy. Rather, the purpose is for everyone to be reminded of their own experience of decline, so that complacency and forgetfulness do not have a chance to set in—to help those in long-term recovery remember the way life was before their own recovery as motivation to stay sober, and to help newcomers identify with their own decline and hopelessness in order to offer a path of hope and renewal.

Attendees only use first names at meetings (and some meetings are "open" meetings, which means they welcome anyone interested in attending, whether they have a substance use disorder or not). The process of mutual sharing is governed by certain procedural traditions. For example, it is customary not to interrupt or question a speaker (cross talking). After a speaker is finished, the group simply expresses its thanks, after which members are free to share their thoughts and feelings based on their own experiences. Speaking one at a time, members may relate to the group that a speaker's talk reminded them of how their own substance use created problems for themselves and their families.

Denial refers to the emotional and intellectual difficulties that people typically encounter in facing a personal limitation or loss. With respect to alcoholism and addiction, denial is a difficulty in facing and accepting the loss of one's control over drinking or using other drugs, as well as the need to give them up for good. Denial is a defining characteristic for those who have severe substance use disorders, since it is difficult to accept the progressive failure of one's own willpower and the loss of one's personal control. Denial has a parallel concept in psychotherapy: resistance. Resistance similarly refers to participants' unwillingness to face the reality of their situation, for example, the participant resisting the idea that his or her substance use is what led to a divorce.

There are common threads in the literature and meetings of fellowships for substance use disorders (such as AA, MA, and NA). In fact, those common threads continue in fellowships for compulsive behaviors (such as Overeaters Anonymous and Gamblers Anonymous). Twelve Step fellowships themselves make no commitment to a particular etiological model of addiction. Rather, they focus on related concepts, such as loss of control and denial. Addiction involves the inability to reliably stop, combined with an unwillingness to accept the reality that personal willpower alone has proven insufficient to arrest the addiction. This is addressed early in *Alcoholics Anonymous* in a description of someone with alcohol use disorder: "Once he takes any alcohol whatever into his system, something happens, both in the bodily and mental sense, which makes it virtually impossible for him to stop."[6] It is similarly addressed in *Narcotics Anonymous:* "We tried limiting our usage to social amounts without success. There is no such thing as a social addict."[7]

Spirituality and Pragmatism

Historically, fellowships like AA reflect on two parallel themes in their programs for recovery—*spirituality* and *pragmatism*. All Twelve Step programs share a commitment to "a Power greater than ourselves" as a key to recovery. Members are encouraged to conceptualize this power in any way they choose, as long as it represents a power greater than their own willpower, which is regarded as insufficient to conquer addiction. This greater power thus represents something in which members may place their hope and faith for the ability to stay sober. For many people, that "power" is the fellowship itself. Spirituality is discussed further in chapter 3 (pages 36–38), chapter 8 (pages 87–96), and chapter 14 (pages 139–43).

Twelve Step fellowships also conceptualize recovery as a process of spiritual renewal, part of which involves a "surrender" to this external power (in contrast to clinging to personal willpower). A description of this experience follows.

> I began turning my will and my life over to the process of recovery and to the spiritual principles that could be found in the steps. I was told to be honest about my belief, even if it was devoid of a god; otherwise the remaining steps would be of no value. I started to have faith in what recovery could offer me. With the strength and courage I

found, I continued. . . . The result was a spiritual awakening, a realization that I could stay clean, work the steps, be an upstanding member of Narcotics Anonymous, have a life worth living, and carry a message of recovery.

—*Narcotics Anonymous*[8]

Despite their strong spiritual base, Twelve Step programs are remarkable for their lack of religious dogma. They promote spirituality in the sense that they advocate values such as honesty, humility, and altruism, as well as activities such as prayer and meditation. Fellowships like AA, MA, and NA are not religious organizations, however. Instead, they are fellowships of individuals connected by a common purpose and guided by common traditions.

Moreover, while spirituality is an important theme in fellowships, so too is a striking pragmatism—the idea that individuals should follow whatever course of action works in order to maintain abstinence. A common saying within Twelve Step fellowships is "Take what works and leave the rest."

Diversity and Democracy

Anyone wishing to implement TSF should be aware of the great diversity that exists within the Twelve Step culture, as this awareness can add to the effectiveness of the program. Today, it is easy, especially in urban centers, to find fellowship groups specifically for women, for men, for the LGBTQ community, for young people, for older people, for clergy, for agnostics and atheists, for nurses or doctors, and so on. There are also Twelve Step groups for any number of cultural and ethnic groups. Looking at the official literature of Twelve Step fellowships reveals themes common to addiction and recovery, but meetings themselves are run differently and vary greatly. This is one reason why newcomers to Twelve Step fellowships are encouraged to "try out" a number of meetings—to explore and find one or more groups where they will feel most comfortable.

The principles of everyone having the same rights and everyone being treated equally are at the heart of Twelve Step fellowships, and that can be seen in the diversity of fellowship groups. By nature, these groups are welcoming, seen in the third of the Twelve Traditions of AA and NA. Furthermore, fellowships manifest a clear and distinct dislike for personal power, embracing instead a strong preference for simple democracy. Consider the following quote from *Twelve Steps and Twelve Traditions*, written when AA was establishing itself as a fellowship: "In the world about us we saw personalities destroying whole peoples. The struggle for wealth, power, and prestige was tearing humanity apart as never before."[9] AA responded to unbridled ambition and radical individualism by creating a fellowship founded on anonymity and governed by simple democratic principles. That ideology is emphasized in the way AA discusses the formation of a new Twelve Step fellowship:

> Being the founder [of a new AA group], he is at first the boss. Who else could be? Very soon, though, his assumed authority to run everything begins to be shared with the first alcoholics he has helped. At this moment, the benign dictator becomes the chairman of a committee composed of his friends. These are the growing group's hierarchy of service—self-appointed, of course, because there is no other way. . . .
>
> Now [after the group has existed for a while] comes the election. If the founder and his friends have served well, they may—to their surprise—be reinstated for a time. If, however, they have heavily resisted the rising tide of democracy, they may be summarily beached. In either case, the group now has a so-called rotating committee, very sharply limited in its authority. In no sense whatever can its members govern or direct the group. They are servants.
>
> —*Twelve Steps and Twelve Traditions*[10]

In fact, the Fourth of the Twelve Traditions addresses the autonomy of individual groups, and the Seventh Tradition discusses each group's financial independence.

No approval is needed from any centralized organization in order to start an AA, MA, NA, or other Twelve Step fellowship meeting; nor are meetings monitored or centrally controlled in any way, for "our Society has no president having authority to govern it, no treasurer who can compel the payment of any dues, no board of directors who can cast an erring member into outer darkness."[11]

With these Traditions to guide them, it should be no surprise that Twelve Step fellowships have adapted well—indeed, proliferated—in an era characterized by the emergence of gender, sexual, and cultural consciousness.

Within this democratic framework, the agenda for a meeting can be whatever the group decides it should be, provided the focus is on staying sober. Some meetings are "speaker" meetings, in which members take turns telling their stories (or invite someone to do so). Other meetings are "discussion" meetings, where the agenda is to share thoughts on some significant theme related to recovery. Some meetings limit their agendas to discussing certain Steps; others focus on a particular book. Some groups emphasize spirituality and prayer, while others prefer to focus on men's or women's issues in recovery, and others still on pragmatic issues such as strategies for avoiding high-risk situations. Many cultural groups have adapted the AA concept of a Higher Power to suit their own religious beliefs and traditions.

The Traditions at the heart of Twelve Step fellowships have fostered a richness and diversity that have made the Twelve Step model accessible to a truly remarkable range of cultural groups. "Twelve Steppers" are connected not only by their common view of addiction—a disorder marked by loss of control and hopelessness for which the only hope to be found is in cooperative effort and mutual support—but also by their traditions of democracy and pluralism.

> What a caring and wonderful family. We love, respect, support, and protect one another. Together, we reach out to newcomers. We sponsor our individual and collective spiritual growth. We carry the NA message of hope and freedom to suffering addicts. And we love and care for one another until we learn to love and care for ourselves.
>
> —*Narcotics Anonymous*[12]

Recovery Dimensions and Change

Treatment and recovery for a substance use disorder can also be understood as a process of change within several *dimensions* of a person's life. The three dimensions focused on in TSF and TSF-COD are social/behavioral, cognitive, and spiritual. A recovery model that includes a focused approach to all three dimensions is useful for facilitators. TSF is facilitated with the assumption that individuals may make changes at different rates in each dimension.

Table 1 presents a schematic approach for change and recovery using TSF recovery dimensions.

Table 1. TSF Recovery Dimensions Change Process

DIMENSION	KEY CONCEPT	CORE PROCESS	MARKERS
Social/Behavioral	Getting active	Building a support network	• Active participation • Sponsor • Home group • Mental health treatment (TSF-COD)
Cognitive	Denial	Acceptance and surrender	• Identifying as a recovering person • Identifying as a person recovering from a co-occurring disorder (TSF-COD) • Acceptance of abstinence as a personal goal • Acceptance of mental health treatment (TSF-COD) • Adherence to a prescription regimen (TSF-COD)
Spiritual	Personal growth	Spiritual awakening	• Moral inventory • Prayer/meditation • Altruism • Spiritual activities

While each recovery dimension is important and deserves therapeutic attention, we theorize that together they offer a balanced, more robust recovery. Therefore, both TSF and TSF-COD focus on making significant changes in all three dimensions. The TSF facilitator may find table 1 useful as a guide for therapeutic efforts and a gauge for participants' recovery. Facilitators using TSF may benefit by monitoring how each dimension is addressed in a participant's treatment plan and in TSF sessions. This will lead to a balanced approach in topics discussed, assigned recovery tasks, and reflection across each of the three recovery dimensions. The recovery dimensions will be covered in more detail in chapter 3.

Correcting Common Misconceptions of TSF

It's helpful to reiterate that TSF is not AA, as the two are often mistakenly confused. TSF is a therapeutic program, conducted in individual or group settings, that addresses substance use disorders as chronic, long-term disorders. TSF involves therapeutic methods such as coaching, role-playing, and dialogue around critical concepts, attitudes, and behaviors. TSF is "psychotherapy-assisted recovery."

Many individuals continue to get into recovery simply by walking into a Twelve Step meeting, without the assistance of a therapist. One might call that "natural" recovery. TSF sessions include information on the Twelve Steps of AA and similar fellowships, with particular focus on the first five Steps. Additionally, individual participants are encouraged to attend fellowship meetings like AA in conjunction with the TSF treatment program.

Alcoholics Anonymous says, "The principles we have set down are guides to progress. We claim spiritual progress rather than spiritual perfection." [13] But AA and its sister fellowships are frequently criticized precisely for seeking perfection—because someone who has a slip is regarded as having failed and now needs to start all over. It must be acknowledged that some individuals may have negative, even toxic, experiences when trying to get involved in a Twelve Step fellowship. This is unavoidable. Fellowships like AA, MA, and NA have no centralized mechanism by which to monitor or correct their members' behavior. There are no set requirements, for example, for becoming a sponsor. For this reason, it is recommended that individuals try out a few different meetings before selecting a group. Twelve Step fellowships do not endorse any sort of hierarchy among their members. On the contrary, by tradition, the newcomer is the most important member at a meeting. The wise and appropriately humble long-timer recognizes this and does not feel superior to or patronize the man or woman who comes to a meeting after a slip.

For some, TSF has negative religious connotations. Although the majority of men and women express positive feelings toward their choice of religion, this is not universally true. Indeed, some individuals with substance use disorders may have experienced exploitation, rejection, or abuse at some point through their participation in organized religion. Such experiences render them understandably skeptical of religion. That is why it is of the utmost importance to emphasize that Twelve Step fellowships advocate values and behaviors that could be called spiritual, but that is different from being a religion. Also, despite the facilitator's personal religious preferences, he or she should not advocate for joining any organized religion as part of implementing TSF.

Another common criticism is that TSF does not work for everyone. This is true. Research has shown that roughly 50 percent of individuals with chronic physical illnesses do not adhere to their doctors' advice regarding treatment, including lifestyle changes and medication. Similarly, estimates are that half of those who try AA stop going within three months. This should not be interpreted to mean that medical treatments (and AA) "fail" half the time, however.

Part of surrendering involves seeking help, and research shows conclusively that TSF, like Twelve Step fellowships, does work for some—particularly those who adhere to the treatment—so it is worth a try. In addition, TSF may be part of a wider therapeutic approach that includes individual, marital, or family therapy, for example. Together, psychotherapy and involvement in a Twelve Step fellowship can be a powerful combination. Combined therapeutic approaches can help people in recovery to identify and deal with issues including trauma, failed attachments, and abuse that may have contributed to initial substance use. As long as additional therapy supports Twelve Step fellowship involvement, the decision to seek psychotherapy is highly recommended. In fact, with trained professional and peer counselors to facilitate involvement in Twelve Step fellowships through education, coaching, and working through resistance together, both TSF and TSF-COD are examples of psychotherapy-assisted recovery.

Volunteer and Peer Facilitation

As stated earlier, the earliest effort to incorporate the Twelve Step model of recovery into formal treatment took place around 1950 at Willmar State Hospital in Minnesota. As part of a multidisciplinary team of staff members, psychologist Dan Anderson, PhD, helped initiate what is now recognized as a reputable, evidence-based treatment model. Part of that treatment approach involved support from peer groups. In addition to these peer groups, Dr. Anderson and his colleagues were assisted by a paraprofessional staff that consisted of men and women in recovery. "It seemed that the mutual assistance and support of other participants facing a similar problem could be utilized by any one of the members of such a group."[14]

It is reasonable to consider what role volunteers and peers can play in implementing a treatment program such as TSF. In this format, we recommend that facilitation be collaborative between a trained professional and one or more peer counselors, similar to the way it was facilitated by Dr. Anderson and his colleagues. The reason for this is that TSF is best conceptualized as psychotherapy-assisted recovery. Some of the activities in the program generally require some degree of training, and treatment plans benefit from the involvement of a qualified professional as a result. However, with assistance from someone qualified, there is no reason why peer-assisted or volunteer-assisted facilitation could not be an effective way to administer TSF. With the TSF-COD program, it is recommended that peer facilitators first receive some form of training and work closely with a mental health professional who is an expert in treating both substance use disorders and mental health disorders.

Medication-Assisted Treatment

The subject of medication-assisted treatment (MAT) can arouse conflicting opinions in Twelve Step fellowships. Some feel that complete abstinence from all drugs is a requirement for recovery. Recovery begins with the decision to stop substance use; however, recovery from any health condition can sometimes require prescribed medication. For this reason, instead of talking about MAT, some talk instead about using medications as an aid in recovery.

Many opinions on the topic are formed out of misinformation. Reasons for prescribing medication in treatment and recovery vary. Some medications assist with withdrawal, others change the way addictive substances affect people, and still others help manage co-occurring mental health disorders, such as depression or anxiety. Medications may play a role in a treatment and recovery plan, and ultimately that is the decision of the participant, with help from his or her doctor, therapist, and Higher Power. Both AA and NA take similar stances on this in their literature. But medications alone are insufficient to achieve lasting recovery.[15] The key is finding a group that welcomes individuals using medication-assisted treatment as part of their treatment or recovery plans. Medication-assisted treatment is discussed further in chapter 8 on pages 91–92.

TSF with Adolescents

Among youth, issues related to identity development can be seriously affected by substance use disorders. Heavy use of alcohol or other drugs inevitably compromises the capacity for adolescents to succeed academically, and it also affects the peer group they identify with. This in turn can lead to limited expectations for the lifestyle they might anticipate as adults. Substance use disorders can cause teens to make less healthy decisions—ones that impact long-term success. Recovery offers the opportunity to set more auspicious goals for the future.

Adolescents sometimes have different needs than adults, and specialized instructions for facilitation of TSF or TSF-COD with adolescents are included in some session descriptions and sections of the handbook and facilitator guides. Not all sessions have special considerations for youth, but they are clearly marked when appropriate.

TSF in Groups

Changes in health care have increased the demand for group-administered services for substance use disorders, a possible advantage for TSF. A review of research comparing substance use treatment in an individual setting versus with group facilitation concluded that individual and group treatment yielded equivalent outcomes.[16]

Group implementation of TSF or TSF-COD is straightforward. An additional advantage to group implementation of TSF is that the Twelve Step model of recovery relies on mutual support groups. A facilitator guides TSF and TSF-COD sessions, but both Twelve Step meetings and TSF sessions are structured. Therefore, group facilitation of TSF in some ways mirrors what participants will encounter attending AA, MA, NA, or other Twelve Step meetings. Group facilitation is discussed in chapter 4 on page 47.

■ ■ ■

3

Recovery Dimensions

In chapter 2, we introduced the concept of recovery dimensions. In effect, what we are suggesting is that recovery may not necessarily proceed along a single, straight path or series of *stages*. Rather, recovery can also be conceptualized as a process that can proceed along several different *dimensions*. This is based on the authors' experience with individuals in recovery. It is not uncommon, for example, to hear someone say that they went to meetings and did not drink or use for a year or more before they were finally able to admit that alcohol or other drugs had made their lives unmanageable (Step One). Considering such experiences, we offer the following schema for looking at recovery as a process that moves along three dimensions. We firmly believe, however, that the most resilient recoveries are grounded in all three dimensions.

Social/Behavioral Dimension of Recovery

The social/behavioral goal of the TSF program is to promote participants' bonding to a fellowship. Markers for this bonding process include progressive participation in meetings and a shift in one's primary social network—away from those who themselves use or support the use of alcohol and other drugs and toward a group that supports sobriety. It should be noted that while TSF is a treatment program, AA and NA are not treatment programs. Rather, their primary goal is relapse prevention. AA and NA exist, first and foremost, to offer group support and practical guidance, primarily in two fundamental recovery areas: how to avoid using alcohol and other drugs, and what to do next if you have a slip. Changing behavior patterns and establishing ties to others who share the same goals have always been central themes for AA and NA. Such network support is a powerful predictor of recovery.[1]

Key Concept: Getting Active

Getting active involves action, or "walking the talk" of recovery. Participants need to recognize how they may have altered their lifestyles over time to accommodate substance use, often at the expense of other activities, and how pursuing alternative habits and routines can help to build a more resilient recovery. This includes attending meetings, participating in meetings, selecting a "home group," getting a sponsor, and building a social network of recovering men and women. Change in this dimension can begin by getting a participant to attend a few different meetings just to listen.

Beginning to attend Twelve Step meetings is a change toward welcoming a new social network. Participants should examine links between their substance use and their current social network (friends, family members, and even intimate significant others), with particular attention on whether those people may be enabling their use. From there, participants may gradually progress to deeper levels of involvement and bonding, eventually including speaking at meetings, getting a sponsor, volunteering for service work, socializing before and/or after meetings, and socializing outside of meetings. Participants will need to either replace the enablers in their lives with supporters or encourage the enablers to change, such as by admitting to their prior enabling efforts. There are many ways to reach out in today's world—over coffee, over the phone, online, or even through mobile apps. Getting active emphasizes how essential building a supportive social network is to recovery. Core Topic 4 and Elective Topic 3 address getting active.

Core Process: Building a Support Network

Participants need to understand how a substance use disorder constitutes a "relationship" with one or more mood-altering substances (and perhaps a behavior such as gambling) that over time can take precedence over relationships with other people, including friends, family, and significant others. Participants may also have encouraged significant others in their lives to "enable" their own alcohol or other drug use, for instance, by helping them obtain alcohol or other drugs, and/or by helping them avoid or minimize the negative consequences of their drinking or using (or gambling).

The support of friends and family, if possible, can be helpful to those in treatment and recovery. In fact, many treatment programs include family involvement. Other support may come from a physician, a psychotherapist or counselor, a spiritual advisor, or other support network. And, of course, central to TSF is the support of Twelve Step fellowships. Building support is addressed in Core Topic 4, Elective Topic 3, and also in the conjoint program.

Markers: Attending Meetings; Sponsorship; Home Group
There are three markers associated with change in the social/behavioral recovery dimension. Markers for social/behavioral change are addressed in Core Topic 4 and Elective Topic 3.

Attending meetings is the first marker of social/behavioral change. A 2014 survey of AA members indicated an average meeting attendance of 2.5 AA meetings per week.[2] Studies show that Twelve Step meeting attendance has a positive correlation with abstinence and long-term recovery.[3]

Sponsorship is the second marker of social/behavioral change. A sponsor is someone the participant can call on (in addition to other fellowship friends) who supports reliance on a fellowship of peers as the bedrock of recovery. Newcomers are encouraged to ask for a "temporary sponsor" as soon as possible, and they should be prepared for that sponsor to be in frequent (often daily) contact. Results of a study published in 2012 showed that individuals in AA who scored high on sponsorship involvement were seven times more likely to remain abstinent than those in the low-sponsorship group, independent of how many meetings they attended.[4]

Belonging to a home group is the third marker of social/behavioral change. A home group is selected by the participant and is defined in the following way:

> Traditionally, most A.A. members through the years have found it important to belong to one group which they call their "Home Group." This is the group where they accept service responsibilities and try to sustain friendships. And although all A.A. members are usually welcome at all groups and feel at home at any of these meetings, the

concept of the "Home Group" has still remained the strongest bond between the A.A. member and the Fellowship.

—*The A.A. Group . . . Where It All Begins*[5]

Cognitive Dimension of Recovery

Recovery can also be measured in terms of changes in one's thinking. The First and Second Steps of AA and NA challenge participants to change their thinking about the role that substance use has played in their lives. This change process moves from *denial* toward *acceptance.* Denial and powerlessness, versus acceptance of reality and positive expectations for change, form the basis for the first two Steps of AA. These in turn set the stage for motivation and behavioral change. Indeed, some argue that behavioral change without cognitive change may reflect mere compliance[6] as opposed to change that is driven by true acceptance and belief.

Emotional states are also an important part of the cognitive recovery dimension. Recognizing that emotions like anger, resentment, loneliness, and shame—which are actually connected to a thought process—can lead to an urge to drink or use other drugs helps to develop strategies for alternative ways of coping with such emotional states. Emotions are discussed in chapter 13 on pages 129–37.

Key Concept: Denial

Participants need to understand some of the ways in which their thinking has been affected by substance use. Drinking and using often lead to rationalizing and lying, to oneself as much as to others. Many with severe substance use disorders deny the reality that alcohol and other drugs have affected their lives in negative ways. They resist admitting the connection between substance use and the accumulating negative consequences that result from it. These consequences may be physical, social, legal, psychological, financial, and spiritual. They ignore how their own rationalizations can contribute to continued drinking or using despite these negative consequences. For example, they may attribute an automobile accident (while driving under the influence) to "bad luck"—or bad tires!

Many with substance use disorders resist making causal attributions concerning their substance use. For instance, a self-employed male with a severe stimulant use disorder may attribute his failing business to a bad economy, unfair competition, or bad employees rather than to his own cocaine-induced mismanagement. Denial and cognitive change are discussed in chapter 7 on pages 77–85.

Core Process: Acceptance and Surrender

By *acceptance*, we mean the breakdown of the illusion that the individual, through willpower alone, can effectively and reliably limit or control his or her use of alcohol and/or other drugs. Acceptance takes several forms in Twelve Step programs:

- acceptance by the participant that he or she suffers from a chronic and progressive disorder characterized by compulsive use of alcohol and/or other drugs

- acceptance by the participant that his or her life is (or is becoming) unmanageable as a result of substance use

- acceptance by the participant that he or she has lost the ability to effectively moderate his or her drinking or using through willpower alone

- acceptance by the participant that since there is no effective way to reliably moderate his or her use, the only reasonable alternative is to pursue abstinence from the use of alcohol and other drugs as his or her goal

Surrender involves a willingness to reach out beyond oneself and to follow the program laid out in the Twelve Steps. Surrender includes acknowledgment by the participant

- that the best hope for recovery—sustained sobriety—is through "coming to believe"; i.e., trusting in some "power" greater than individual willpower

- that such a "power" exists in the form of fellowships for those with substance use problems

- that his or her best chances for success are to "work the Steps" and become actively involved in a fellowship

Markers: Identifying as a Recovering Person; Acceptance of Abstinence as a Personal Goal

Acceptance in recovery often contributes to a person's sense of *identity*, specifically as a *recovering* individual. Researchers studying this issue have found that individuals who identified themselves as *recovering* addicts or alcoholics fared better with respect to staying abstinent than did a group who merely identified themselves as addicts or alcoholics.[7] For some, this cognitive change may come easily, while others may resist identifying with recovery for some time. The process of moving away from denial and toward acceptance and surrender has proven to be beneficial, which is why identifying with recovery and establishing the goal of abstinence both serve as key markers toward cognitive change.

Spiritual Dimension of Recovery

Although the primary focus of Twelve Step support groups is relapse prevention, the founders of AA believed that alcoholism is a spiritual as well as a physical disorder, and they were keenly interested in healing the spiritual wounds caused by addiction. AA literature does not identify spiritual malaise as a cause of addiction so much as a consequence of it. Accordingly, Steps Three through Twelve of AA and NA could accurately be described as a blueprint for personal insight, growth, and healing—which the AA founders believed went hand in hand with having a "spiritual awakening." TSF does not provide guidelines for helping participants explore all Twelve Steps. It does, however, provide guidelines for exploring spiritual concepts and values such as altruism, honesty, humility (as opposed to arrogance), and the power of meditation or prayer, as well as reading spiritually oriented materials.

In one study, researchers assessed a large group of individuals who had undergone treatment for alcohol use disorders (moderate to severe) with respect to "spirituality" including prayer, meditation, reading spiritual writings, and attending religious services. They found that those who scored higher on spirituality were more likely to remain sober and also likely to drink less if they did have a slip.[8] Spirituality is discussed in chapter 8 on pages 87–96 and in chapter 14 on pages 139–43.

Key Concept: Personal Growth

Participants need to experience hope that they can arrest their substance use disorders. They also need to develop a belief and trust in some power greater than their own willpower—a fellowship of peers seeking a common goal, for example. Isolation and alienation are common with severe substance use disorders, but spiritual change offers an alternative: a belief in the power of honesty, a connection to others, and altruism. Personal growth results from changes in other recovery dimensions as well, so this key concept is addressed throughout the TSF and TSF-COD programs.

Core Process: Spiritual Awakening

A spiritual awakening is part of Step Twelve in the Twelve Steps and therefore may not be fully addressed by the participant during facilitation of TSF or TSF-COD. However, the process of spiritual change is discussed, and the TSF program introduces key concepts for initiating this spiritual change process. The particular manner in which an individual chooses to think of a power greater than the self is up to the individual. But Twelve Step fellowships are founded on the assumption that recovery begins with acceptance of the limitation of one's own willpower, combined with a leap of faith in some greater source of strength.

Markers: Moral Inventory; Prayer/Meditation; Altruism;
Spiritual Activities

There are four markers associated with change in the spiritual dimension. Some of these markers may not be completed by the end of the TSF program, but the core process of a spiritual awakening is discussed in chapter 8, and the key concept of personal growth is discussed in both core and elective topics.

A moral inventory is the first marker of spiritual change. Through their Steps, literature, and Traditions, Twelve Step fellowships like AA, MA, and NA are rich in support that can help to transform a life of hopelessness and moral compromise into one of hope that is built on self-respect and honesty. But the participant must be open to it. Steps Four and Five of the Twelve Steps involve a moral inventory, but that kind of moral inventory is best attempted by an individual who has been abstinent and actively working a Twelve Step program for six months to a year and who has a sponsor. In this facilitation program, the emphasis is on starting to pursue the spiritual dimension of recovery. A moral inventory, in contrast, is limited to accepting responsibility for some of the negative consequences of substance use and discussing some of the guilt or shame associated with that. While the participant will likely focus on the marker of a moral inventory after facilitation of the program is complete, TSF's introduction to a Higher Power and the incorporation of personal growth are important first steps along the road to spiritual change.

Prayer or meditation is the second marker of spiritual change. Both are integral to Step Eleven of the Twelve Steps and are discussed in chapter 14 on page 141.

Altruism is the third marker of spiritual change. The concept of altruism is important in Step Twelve of the Twelve Steps and in the tradition of "giving back to get." Altruism is a movement away from the selfish behaviors common with severe substance use disorders, and thus acts of selflessness are important markers of a spiritual awakening and of personal growth.

■ ■ ■

PART 2

Twelve Step Facilitation Program Overview

4

Structure and Format

TSF and TSF-COD are divided into core and elective topics. In addition, a two-session conjoint program is available (see part 5 on page 179). Both TSF and TSF-COD include a structured termination session. Both programs can be implemented in either a series of individual or group sessions. We recommend that sessions be held weekly or more frequently, depending on the clinical setting, in order to maintain therapeutic "momentum." Implementation of TSF is discussed in part 3, and implementation of TSF-COD is discussed in part 4. The principles remain the same in both programs, however.

Program Structure

Although TSF is designed to allow for flexibility in treatment planning, program facilitation is intended to be implemented in a fairly structured manner. Indeed, maintaining the structure of TSF sessions is essential, whether facilitated individually or in a group format. Additionally, each session should focus on a specific topic.

The session topic (core, elective, and so on) should be determined by the facilitator in advance. The selection of a topic choice should be based on participant (or group) progress to date and what would be the most helpful topic to cover at that time.

First Session

The first session is unique in that the facilitator provides an overview of the entire program (including the goal of active involvement in a Twelve Step fellowship like AA or NA). The facilitator also provides an assessment of the participant's alcohol and/or other drug involvement, introduces the way Twelve Step fellowships view addiction, defines the respective roles and responsibilities of the facilitator and the participant, and attempts to engage the participant's motivation to stay sober. Within the TSF-COD program, this first session also emphasizes the recovery goals for substance use disorders and co-occurring mental health disorders. Both the first session and the termination session have slightly different formats than the rest of the program sessions.

Core Program

The TSF core program consists of sessions covering four topics: Assessment, Acceptance, Surrender, and Getting Active in Twelve Step Fellowships. TSF-COD adds Getting Active in Mental Health Treatment to its core program. It is recommended that the core topics be covered for all participants, regardless of any prior treatment or experience with Twelve Step fellowships. For participants who have undergone a thorough assessment prior to referral to TSF, the assessment session may be abbreviated. However, it is still essential for the facilitator to hear from participants to learn about their substance use histories (and, in TSF-COD, their psychiatric histories) as well as their reasons for seeking treatment now.

Elective Program

The TSF elective program consists of five topics: Genograms; Enabling; People, Places, and Routines; Emotions; and Spirituality. In TSF-COD, the elective topics include Barriers to Getting Active in Twelve Step Fellowships; Barriers to Mental Health Treatment; People, Places, and Routines; Emotions; and Living for Recovery.

The elective program is designed to be more flexible in order to tailor individual treatment plans to the individual participant or group. Assessing progress in the recovery dimensions on an ongoing basis can inform which elective topics are recommended. In addition, a facilitator can extend a topic (core or elective) over more than one session. This is particularly true when implementing TSF in a group format. Finally, a facilitator may repeat a topic at some point if it seems appropriate.

Termination

Completion of the program is an important event. It involves an assessment by both the participant and the facilitator, as well as the setting of future goals. Similar to the first session, the final session has a unique format that is different from the rest of the sessions. This session includes an assessment of the participant's progress, as well as an overall evaluation of the program. Since recovery is an ongoing, lifelong process, and since slips and relapses are a common phenomenon in this process, the termination session also intends to establish ongoing recovery goals and to leave the door open to booster sessions in the future.

Facilitator Guides

Step-by-step instructions for program implementation are included in *Twelve Step Facilitation Facilitator Guide* and *Twelve Step Facilitation for Co-occurring Disorders Facilitator Guide*. The introduction to the guides provides an overview of the respective program and answers frequently asked questions. Instructions for each topic include information on needed materials and preparations, session goals and learner outcomes, necessary background information, suggested time allotments for each activity, and the recovery dimensions that each topic addresses. Suggestions for what facilitators can say out loud are clearly marked, as are instructions for adolescent or group implementation.

Checklists

Both *Twelve Step Facilitation Facilitator Guide* and *Twelve Step Facilitation for Co-occurring Disorders Facilitator Guide* come with a CD-ROM containing reproducible session checklists that can be used both as guidelines for the facilitation of TSF and TSF-COD sessions and as monitoring tools for TSF and TSF-COD treatment fidelity. The checklists also appear at the end of each topic within the guides.

Participant Workbooks

Participants use *Twelve Step Facilitation Workbook* or *Twelve Step Facilitation for Co-occurring Disorders Workbook* to complete exercises related to the TSF or TSF-COD session topics, as well as to document their experiences in recovery and their involvement with Twelve Step fellowships. Using the workbook reinforces participation and continued sobriety by providing space to reflect on fellowship meetings, recovery literature, and slips, as well as to track days abstinent. Each participant should receive his or her own workbook, and these can be purchased separately.

Video

Both the TSF and TSF-COD programs include video as an integral part of program facilitation. Video segments are short and present information on program topics that include the expertise of author Joseph Nowinski and the personal stories of others in recovery. Inclusion of the video is not required in program facilitation, but it is highly recommended that the video be used. Instructions for where to play the video segments are included in the facilitator guide, along with recommended follow-up questions for discussion. There are two separate videos, one for the TSF program and one for the TSF-COD program.

Session Format

All sessions follow a similar format, beginning with a review of the previous week's experiences, proceeding to a presentation of new material, and ending with the assignment of recovery tasks. Each topic includes a structured step-by-step outline that includes instructions for activities as well as suggested scripts for presenting key concepts.

A central part of the TSF and TSF-COD programs is consistent encouragement for participants to attend Twelve Step meetings on a regular basis and to become involved in fellowship rather than merely observing. Participants should be encouraged to experiment with a variety of meetings (e.g., Step meetings, speaker meetings, men's or women's meetings) and to eventually commit to a home group for meetings. Participants are also encouraged to read Twelve Step fellowships' World Service literature during the course of the program (e.g., *Alcoholics Anonymous, Narcotics Anonymous,* or *Twelve Steps and Twelve Traditions*).

Review

All sessions except the first begin with the facilitator checking in with participants. This means briefly reviewing their experiences since the last session and following up on any recovery tasks, with special emphasis on sober days, slips, meetings attended, and networking. This review at the opening of each session is crucial. By focusing on what participants have done since the last TSF session, the facilitator sets the expectation for action and establishes that together the facilitator and the participant will follow up on those expectations in future sessions.

Recovery tasks discussed at the end of the previous session are an important part of the review. The participant or group should be asked not just if the tasks were completed, but what those experiences were like. If individuals did not complete any recovery tasks, the facilitator should encourage individuals to discuss why they were not completed. Due to limited time in the sessions, discussions regarding recovery tasks should be focused on the tasks themselves and why they were or were not completed. Collateral issues (e.g., problems related to work or school, relationships, or children) can be acknowledged, but the purpose of the review is to focus on recovery progress since the last session. For those in the TSF-COD program, recovery tasks include getting active in both Twelve Step fellowships and psychiatric treatment.

During the review, days abstinent should be recognized and positively encouraged. Progress toward sobriety and abstinence deserves sincere congratulations—even if it is given to only one or two members of a group. For participants with co-occurring disorders, recognition should also be given to those who report adherence to their psychiatric treatment—for example, taking medications as prescribed and keeping appointments with prescribers and/or therapists.

Participants who report attending one or more fellowship meetings should be asked to briefly share those experiences, with an emphasis on identifying positive takeaways. In group facilitation of TSF, this can be especially helpful since others may find encouragement in those positive experiences and may be interested in attending meetings with the identified fellowship group.

Urges to drink or use, as well as any slips, should be discussed openly. Slips—times when the participant drank or used in between periods of sobriety—need to be approached nonjudgmentally and should be discussed as events that can be learned from in order to encourage participants to be honest about them. Slips can also be thought of as times when the attraction of substance use overcame a participant's willpower.

Finally, the review should include a discussion about participant reactions to any readings that he or she may have completed since the last TSF session. Participants who consistently report no meeting attendance and/or rejection of psychiatric recommendations should be challenged by the facilitator to explain why, since these are action steps that are important to the success of both TSF and recovery.

New Material

Following the review, each session moves on to cover the core or elective topic's new material. The content of each core and elective topic is described in later chapters, including the relevance of each topic to the overall program and common issues that arise in the facilitation of a given topic.

The core and elective topics introduce the main principles of TSF, and through discussion and activities, the facilitator educates, coaches, and works through resistance. Regardless of whether participants have attended Twelve Step meetings in the past, the participant may not have a thorough understanding of the main principles of Twelve Step recovery. While attending meetings can be a good way to learn more about the Twelve Steps, individuals may not ask questions that can help clarify key concepts and therefore may not understand the full meaning behind them. The main goal of the facilitator presenting new material is to guide a participant through the initial stages of recovery by providing information and inviting discussion. Additionally, the facilitator can explain the research behind the material, which adds validity to content. Peer counselors who are themselves in recovery also benefit from the evidence offered in the research, which lends credibility to their own experience and provides justification to assigned recovery tasks.

In both individual and group formats, the facilitator may opt to continue discussion of a core or elective topic over more than one TSF session. In these instances, it is still vital to end each session with recovery tasks.

Recovery Tasks

Each session should end with the facilitator assigning recovery tasks—suggested work for participants to perform between sessions. These tasks include

- attending mutually agreed-upon Twelve Step meetings
- reading suggested conference-approved literature or other material recommended by the facilitator

- reviewing and completing work in the workbook

- getting active in other ways, such as asking for a temporary sponsor, asking a fellowship member for a phone number or email address, or looking for a home group

- communicating with a prescriber about the effectiveness of medications or undesirable side effects (TSF-COD program)

Recovery tasks should be followed up on at the beginning of the next TSF session. This is very important, as it helps to establish therapeutic momentum by communicating that the facilitator has specific expectations for participants. A therapeutic work ethic establishes the idea that recovery demands action. In a group format, it may not be possible to follow up with every participant in a given session. In that case, we recommend that the facilitator choose different participants to follow up with each time.

Group Format

Increased demand for clinical treatment services has led treatment centers to deliver more therapeutic services in groups, expanding upon traditional, individualized treatment approaches. Research comparing individual and group treatment for substance use disorders shows that both treatment approaches yielded equivalent outcomes.[1]

Because TSF and TSF-COD involve participation in mutual support groups, it may actually be an advantage to have both programs implemented in a group format. Group facilitation of TSF and TSF-COD will mirror what participants encounter when attending Twelve Step fellowship meetings, so the structure will be complementary and familiar. Both TSF and TSF-COD are guided by a facilitator, however, which is a slightly different format than Twelve Step mutual support groups. Nonetheless, group implementation should be familiar to participants, and facilitation is fairly straightforward.

Group Size

Following the previously discussed structure and format, group facilitation optimally involves six to eight participants in session lengths of ninety minutes each. Many clinical settings limit group sessions to sixty minutes, however. Because of this, the sessions may need to be modified slightly. For example, it may be necessary to limit the number of group members who speak during the review portion of the session while others listen. This is similar to Twelve Step meetings in that every member does not typically speak at every meeting. Group members who were quieter or more reserved will therefore likely be prompted to speak up at future meetings so that, over time, recovery efforts for the week are shared by everyone in the group. Some members may experience social anxiety, particularly in the TSF-COD program, and those members will likely need more encouragement to share with the group. For this reason, a more gradual participation is expected for some participants. For more information on how to help participants who struggle with social anxiety, see pages 161–62 in chapter 17.

When introducing new material during the sessions, it may be necessary to break up the content into more than one session. This is perfectly acceptable, as long as the same format is adhered to during each session by including a review, the discussion of new material, and the assigning of recovery tasks. If all of the planned new material does not get discussed, the group can pick up the discussion during the new material part of the next session, but time should still be reserved to discuss recovery tasks before completing the session.

Recovery Tasks

At the end of each TSF or TSF-COD session, the participants should be assigned recovery tasks to complete before the next session. For every session, discussion of recovery tasks for the coming week should include how many Twelve Step fellowship meetings participants are willing to attend, pertinent readings in conference-approved and other published literature, and any other tasks that may help to support and solidify recovery efforts. Some recovery efforts will be assigned to the entire group (such as suggested passages from basic texts), while more specific tasks may be assigned to individuals. During group facilitation, the specific recovery tasks assigned to some of the participants may be highlighted in order to call attention to how individuals approach and manage recovery tasks. In subsequent sessions, different members should be selected so that eventually the recovery progress of everyone in the group is discussed. Facilitation of the TSF and TSF-COD topics includes the use of participant workbooks. During group sessions, the workbooks can guide discussion around session topics and recovery tasks for the following week; members take the workbooks with them and complete them individually prior to the next session.

Promoting Group Cohesion

Another benefit of group facilitation for TSF and TSF-COD is that it generally promotes group cohesion, which can in turn promote recovery. For example, participants may volunteer to attend meetings together. This should be encouraged. When in a group setting, individuals should also be encouraged to share information with the group about meetings they attended that they found particularly helpful. Other group members may be looking for more supportive groups to attend, and sharing in this way can help recovery efforts. Participants should, however, be discouraged from sharing the same sponsor.

It can be advantageous for individuals to simply listen to other members in group facilitation as well. Listening is actually a core element of Twelve Step recovery. Members may learn by listening, and what they hear may turn into action. Shy or anxious participants can be gradually encouraged to speak. Resistant participants still hear what is being said, and the positive experiences of others may influence them sooner or later.

Rolling Admissions and Standing Groups

There is no requirement that participants begin or end TSF as a group. Newcomers are welcomed at all Twelve Step meetings and are sometimes given special attention as people who are possibly looking for support. Newcomers to TSF and TSF-COD groups should be welcomed as well. In Twelve Step fellowships, a newcomer may be given a quick explanation of the "rules of the road" for that group's meeting structure. In both the TSF and TSF-COD programs, a new participant should be informed of rules and decorum prior to attending a session group meeting. The participants should be advised of the TSF session format and structure, including the fact that sessions are guided by a facilitator. The importance of recovery tasks should also be explained and stressed. A participant's first session of TSF or TSF-COD should involve introducing himself or herself to the group and sharing the reasons for participating in the program.

The core topics for TSF and TSF-COD are progressive and should therefore be done in order; however, the elective topics are designed to be more flexible and rolling admissions are welcome (meaning new members could join groups for these topics at any time). Additionally, virtually all topics in the program can be administered in standing groups—ongoing groups that focus on a single topic. In this way, a participant may be exposed to the same TSF topic many times, especially if that topic appears particularly relevant to that individual. Core Topic 2: Acceptance is a good example because the impact may differ in a participant's first, second, or third meeting, depending on where he or she is at in the course of treatment. Other topics that are suitable for standing groups include Core Topic 4: Getting Active in Twelve Step Fellowships; Elective Topic 3: People, Places, and Routines; and Elective Topic 4: Emotions. Again, this is similar to Twelve Step meetings, where the same topic or Step may be the subject of multiple meetings that an individual may attend. Step meetings, for example, focus on a single Step or set of Steps as the subject of each meeting.

Conference-Approved Literature

Since their inception, Twelve Step fellowships have emphasized the value of published literature to people in recovery or trying to embrace sobriety. The primary documents that have emerged through the fellowships (often referred to as "basic texts") provide an understanding of these fellowships, views of addiction and recovery, and the main ideas at the heart of these organizations. These texts are seen as an integral part of the recovery process. Reading and sharing the primary texts developed and published by each organization's fellowship is often part of regular fellowship meetings and is recommended to anyone in recovery. In addition to publishing these primary documents, many Twelve Step organizations publish other literature and audiovisual materials, seen as a complementary bibliotherapy program to support personal growth and reflection. While there is a significant number of resources available to assist with recovery efforts, the term *conference-approved* refers to resources that have been approved for publication by the Twelve Step organization to which they refer.

Facilitation of the TSF and TSF-COD programs includes recommended reading for participants. Depending on individual participant needs and circumstances, the recommended reading materials may vary. Table 2 lists some of the largest Twelve Step organizations and some of the main literature recommended to members. For more information, visit the websites for each organization. Facilitators should encourage participants involved in TSF to obtain literature and engage in the recommended reading.

Table 2. Twelve Step Fellowship Literature

ORGANIZATION	LITERATURE
Alcoholics Anonymous	*Alcoholics Anonymous* ("Big Book") *Twelve Steps and Twelve Traditions* ("Twelve and Twelve") *Daily Reflections*
Cocaine Anonymous	*Narcotics Anonymous* *Hope, Faith and Courage* *Twelve Steps and Twelve Traditions* *A Quiet Peace*
Emotions Anonymous	*Emotions Anonymous* *It Works If You Work It* *Today*
Gamblers Anonymous	*Sharing Recovery Through Gamblers Anonymous* *A New Beginning* ("Red Book") *A Day at a Time*
Marijuana Anonymous	*Life with Hope*
Narcotics Anonymous	*Narcotics Anonymous* *It Works: How and Why* ("Green and Gold") *Just for Today*

Table 2. Twelve Step Fellowship Literature (*cont.*)

ORGANIZATION	LITERATURE
Nicotine Anonymous	*Nicotine Anonymous* *90 Days, 90 Ways* *A Year of Miracles*
Overeaters Anonymous	*Overeaters Anonymous* *The Twelve Steps and Twelve Traditions of Overeaters Anonymous*
Sex Addicts Anonymous	*Sex Addicts Anonymous* ("Green Book") *Voices of Recovery*

■ ■ ■

5

Facilitator Guidelines

Role of the Facilitator

The facilitator's first responsibility with a participant is to administer an assessment to gain information about the participant's history of use, to determine whether a substance use disorder is indicated (and how severe), to determine whether there are any co-occurring mental health concerns, and to develop an individualized treatment plan. Assessment is a core topic of the TSF and TSF-COD program and is discussed in chapter 6 on pages 65–75. If the initial assessment indicates a moderate to severe substance use disorder—and if it also reveals several unsuccessful attempts to stop or control use—then TSF (or TSF-COD) should be suggested to the participant as an appropriate treatment option.

Familiarity and comfort with Twelve Step culture is essential to successful facilitation of TSF or TSF-COD, and one of the most important goals of both programs is active involvement in a Twelve Step fellowship. With TSF-COD, active involvement with mental health treatment is also a goal. Facilitation of both TSF and TSF-COD is best done by a licensed professional, perhaps working in concert with a trained peer counselor. One advantage of utilizing trained peer counselors is that they may be free to engage in activities that licensed professionals may not, such as accompanying participants to Twelve Step fellowship meetings. In some clinical settings, peer counselors may actively participate in TSF sessions or merely sit and observe them.

Education and Advocacy

There are many ways in which the facilitator acts as both an educational resource and an advocate of the Twelve Step approach to recovery.

It's important that the participant get a thorough explanation of how Twelve Step fellowships view addiction—as chronic, progressive conditions marked by loss of control (inability to stop or consistently moderate use). The participant should receive help assessing how substance use disorders (and untreated mental disorders, if appropriate) relate to consequences in his or her life. These consequences may be legal or financial, or they may affect health (injury, stamina, medical conditions, and so on), school or work performance, family life, and emotional stability (mood swings, ability to concentrate, depression, or irritability).

The participant may exhibit signs of denial in his or her attitude toward drinking or using (and possibly untreated mental illness), and these should be discussed. Other important topics for discussion include several of the Twelve Steps and their related concepts. It is important to help the participant to understand key Twelve Step themes and concepts (such as denial and unmanageability) as they are reflected in his or her own life experiences.

Facilitation should introduce, explain, and advocate for reliance on Twelve Step fellowships as the foundation for recovery, including how to develop a support network through participation in Twelve Step fellowship activities and online networking. Sponsorship should be explained, including what to look for in a sponsor. Recovery should be explained as an ongoing process for healthy management of substance use disorders, not as a process for curing addiction. Questions may arise about material found in Twelve Step group literature or other readings, and the facilitator should answer those to the best of his or her ability.

Coaching

Certain aspects of a participant's recovery will need to be monitored, such as the progression toward greater involvement with Twelve Step fellowships as a way to maintain abstinence. Progression in this sense can be measured by the participant's willingness to attend meetings that require more personal involvement, such as Step meetings and closed-discussion meetings rather than open-speaker meetings. Other measures include showing willingness to attend a variety of meetings in order to choose a home group, asking for a temporary sponsor, showing willingness to volunteer for basic service work (making coffee, setting up for or cleaning up after meetings, and so on), and finding appropriate Twelve Step fellowship social events to attend. Participants should also be encouraged to get contact information from other fellowship group members, such as phone numbers and email addresses, so that they can contact each other between meetings. Developing a network of recovering friends is a desirable long-term goal.

A facilitator can help a participant to locate Twelve Step fellowship meetings and provide encouragement to attend and participate. This can be accomplished in a variety of ways, including tackling problem-solving issues together, such as transportation and child care. Role-playing can help make a participant more comfortable in a number of different scenarios, such as asking meeting attendees for phone numbers, volunteering to help with setup or cleanup at meetings, approaching potential sponsors, and more. Peer counselors may even offer to attend initial meetings with the participant and discuss them afterward.

The participant may also need assistance with sponsorship. Understanding the role of a sponsor is important, and participants may need encouragement to seek temporary sponsorship in early recovery until a more permanent sponsor can be found. Recovery tasks offer another opportunity to focus on successful integration into Twelve Step fellowships.

Empathy and Caring Detachment
A good facilitator of TSF will both empathize with the participant and maintain caring detachment. Empathy is important when building rapport with a participant, in the process of identifying denial, and during the struggle with acceptance. An important part of facilitation is empathizing with the participants' feelings of shame, anger, anxiety, and guilt over substance use and the problems it has caused. It is also important to be able to identify with resistance to the idea of abstinence (denial) and with feelings of loss associated with having to give up alcohol and other drugs. Empathy can help more than confrontation to facilitate "saying good-bye" to substance use and embracing abstinence.

But caring detachment is also important. For example, supporting a participant after a slip should involve analyzing that slip and taking actions to get and remain sober. It needs to be communicated to a participant that he or she must do whatever it takes to remain abstinent. Time spent sober should be recognized, thereby reinforcing ongoing progress toward abstinence. Participants transitioning to sobriety should begin to reflect on longstanding issues and wounds that may have contributed to their substance use, if only initially. The facilitator needs to offer support, yet encourage the participant to begin dealing with those issues.

A Collaborative Relationship

A collaborative and supportive relationship with the participant is an important objective of TSF and TSF-COD. Indeed, some bonding between participant and facilitator is appropriate, as it is in any psychotherapy. Facilitation should be engaging, conversational, empathetic, and nonjudgmental. A frank but respectful approach is most likely to facilitate engagement on the part of the participant.

In the complex and stressful psychosocial climate that addiction creates, the participant-facilitator relationship represents an island of sorts. It is a prototype for the kind of relationships that the participant will hopefully cultivate over time through fellowship—relationships that will endure after the participant-facilitator relationship ends. Successful management of the relationship between a participant and facilitator therefore requires an ability to balance genuine care with healthy detachment. The need for facilitator empathy and concern has been noted, but the facilitator cannot come to represent the participant's complete recovery program. The participant-facilitator relationship may be the first "successful" relationship that the participant has had for many years. Even a brief relationship with a facilitator can represent a true watershed in many participants' lives.

This is why discussing the Twelve Steps and encouraging involvement with Twelve Step fellowships is so important. A collaborative and supportive approach in participant-facilitator dynamics will help a participant feel more comfortable establishing relationships with fellowship members and seeking support in recovery through sustained, successful relationships. A facilitator with familiarity and appreciation for Twelve Step Traditions and culture will be able to offer a collaborative relationship that also encourages the development of many more supportive relationships through Twelve Step fellowship.

Focus

This program aims to facilitate change in a relatively short period of time. In settings where there is a limited number of available clinical resources, it becomes a therapeutic challenge for the facilitator to understand the circumstances in a participant's case and cover as much ground as possible in the time available. This requires the facilitator to stay on task and deliver focused treatment.

Achieving sobriety can bring other issues to the surface for participants. Substance use and unhealthy behaviors may be a participant's way of coping with those issues, and the issues themselves are important to address. At the beginning of each TSF or TSF-COD session, a participant may talk about how other issues have impacted his or her week. As difficult as it may be to set aside those concerns and not "follow the participant," it is the facilitator's responsibility to keep sessions focused on the recovery-related issues in the core and elective sessions and to maintain the structure of the TSF and TSF-COD programs.

It may be helpful to use the AA slogan "First things first" with the participant. It can be explained that the "first thing" is to attain a degree of sobriety, with that as the foundation for all other change and growth. In fact, sobriety very well may seem to "spontaneously" resolve some other issues, but there are others it may not resolve. Other issues are very important, and it may help to resolve those issues concurrently with TSF and TSF-COD. But those issues need to be given attention through concurrent psychotherapy (or later on), not during the TSF and TSF-COD sessions.

Agent of Change

The primary agents of long-term change, as seen through the lens of TSF and TSF-COD, are Twelve Step fellowships, not the individual facilitator. That said, the importance of effective facilitation cannot be dismissed or minimized. But facilitation of TSF or TSF-COD is meant to coincide with ongoing Twelve Step support, and fellowship should be the main force responsible for recovery. The facilitated program sessions will come to an end; the support of fellowship should not. Research supports the value of concurrent treatment and Twelve Step meeting attendance,[1] and previously cited research shows that progressive involvement in a fellowship is a predictor of long-term recovery.

In working through the TSF or TSF-COD program, helping a participant to deal with a crisis will doubtless require support from the facilitator. The facilitator may even see the need to schedule an emergency session in order to help deal with the crisis. But the goals of an emergency session should be to help the participant assess the crisis in terms of how it threatens his or her recovery, to consider options consistent with Twelve Step Traditions and establish priorities ("First things first"), to determine what actions can be taken immediately in order to stay sober, and to solve the crisis by relying on Twelve Step resources (meetings, sponsor, Twelve Step literature, other fellowship members, and so on).

As the primary agent of change, involvement with Twelve Step fellowship should be progressive and should involve attending a variety of regular meetings, attending fellowship activities, maintaining regular contact over the telephone or Internet with friends in Twelve Step fellowship groups, and developing a relationship with a sponsor. In future times of crisis, and in terms of regular ongoing support, the participant should be encouraged to rely more upon Twelve Step fellowship resources than on the facilitator. It may even be helpful to point out to the participant that the TSF or TSF-COD program will come to an end and the facilitator will no longer be available for support at that point.

Slogans

Twelve Step fellowships are both spiritual and pragmatic in their approaches to staying sober. Many slogans are commonly shared among members of Twelve Step fellowship groups, and they carry both practical and spiritual significance.

The TSF or TSF-COD program facilitator should be familiar with some of the more popular slogans and be prepared to use them in facilitation, both to promote involvement in Twelve Step fellowships and to offer participants helpful phrases to reflect upon in difficult situations. The better a participant understands the meaning of each slogan, the better he or she will be at applying it on a day-to-day basis.

Another way to think of slogans is that they are consistent with cognitive-behavioral therapy, which is based in part on the notion that what an individual thinks affects that individual's behavior. Thinking about these slogans may alter the way a participant will act in certain situations, and that is part of the change process. A few key Twelve Step slogans are described here. Many more can be found in conference-approved literature and by attending meetings.

"First Things First"

If a participant with a moderate to severe substance use disorder does not maintain abstinence, no other issues in his or her life are likely to be successfully resolved. For example, a decision to seek marriage or family counseling while the participant continues to drink or use other drugs is not likely to prove beneficial. Indeed, individuals whose primary problem is a substance use disorder may be tempted to regard it as secondary to or resultant from some other issue: marital conflict, family conflict, depression, or an unsatisfying career.

Within Twelve Step fellowships, it is generally accepted that this represents a form of denial—that many collateral problems are actually the results of a substance use disorder, not its cause. Listening to the stories told at speaker meetings—*how it was, what happened, and how it is now*—attests to how other issues will arise when recovery begins, and how those issues can only be resolved by an individual who is in recovery as opposed to one caught in the throes of addiction.

"One Day at a Time"

Recovery is best thought of as a journey undertaken one step at a time. The participant's goal is to avoid substance use altogether and permanently, but to do so "One day at a time." Anniversaries of sobriety are important, but what is most important is maintaining sobriety today, not yesterday or tomorrow. This slogan sets the stage for recognizing even a single day of sobriety following a slip or relapse.

"Fake It Till You Make It"

Not everything that a newcomer hears at Twelve Step fellowship meetings will appeal to him or her, and some of it may not make sense either. However, rather than dismissing or challenging those ideas or suggestions, this slogan teaches newcomers and skeptics alike to be humble enough to simply follow advice on faith at first, with the belief that it will prove beneficial in the long run. This includes going to meetings, working the Steps, doing what one's sponsor advises, and so on.

A good example of this is the common suggestion to get a sponsor early and to maintain frequent contact with that sponsor, via email, telephone, messaging, or face-to-face contact. Sponsors often ask newly recovering people to make brief daily contact. They are asked to do this regardless of how they are feeling, and whether or not they have stayed sober. Those in early recovery sometimes don't see the purpose of checking in and may even resent having to do it. They may consider the value of a sponsorship as limited, such as a person to call on in times of distress (for example, during an intense craving or after a slip). But the true purpose of a sponsor is to build a relationship that can endure during good times and bad—one that can serve as a prototype for other relationships that support recovery, as opposed to relationships that enable substance use.

"Easy Does It"

A person in recovery needs to learn how to cope with stress without resorting to substance use. Our society increasingly promotes "compensatory" substance use—the use of mood-altering drugs to reduce anxiety and frustration. Advertisements for psychotropic medications abound in mass media.

This slogan urges someone in recovery to manage stress by limiting its sources: by avoiding "overloading the plate" and by learning to manage stress in healthy ways. Twelve Step fellowships advocate prayer and meditation. Indeed, methods such as mindfulness meditation have become popular as well among advocates of harm reduction, whose goal is returning to low-risk substance use.

"Live and Let Live"

This slogan advises someone in recovery to accept that which cannot be changed, as opposed to trying to "play God," which only creates stress. Things that are sometimes better accepted than challenged include the reality of one's own substance use disorder, certain family or marital problems, other people's personalities, past mistakes and transgressions, decisions that have already been made, situations that must be endured, and injustices that must be suffered. Other Twelve Step fellowship members can offer support with these issues, and this slogan can help remind people to reach out. Managing stress with support can help individuals to get on with their own lives and stop trying to control things they cannot control.

■ ■ ■

PART 3

Twelve Step Facilitation
Treatment Guidelines

>>

Twelve Step Facilitation Treatment Guidelines

TSF consists of a core program and an elective program. These in turn are divided into recovery-related topics as follows:

Core Program

- Chapter 6: Core Topic 1: Assessment
- Chapter 7: Core Topic 2: Acceptance
- Chapter 8: Core Topic 3: Surrender
- Chapter 9: Core Topic 4: Getting Active in Twelve Step Fellowships

Elective Program

- Chapter 10: Elective Topic 1: Genograms
- Chapter 11: Elective Topic 2: Enabling
- Chapter 12: Elective Topic 3: People, Places, and Routines
- Chapter 13: Elective Topic 4: Emotions
- Chapter 14: Elective Topic 5: Spirituality

- Termination

It is important that the facilitator understand that the core and elective topics are not intended to be static exercises; rather, they represent dynamic processes in recovery. For example, the Recovery Lifestyle Contract that is central to Elective Topic 3 is intended to evolve over time as a consequence of reflections and changes. The structure of TSF and TSF-COD intentionally includes follow-ups to monitor these processes as they evolve.

■ ■ ■

6

Core Topic 1: Assessment

The primary purpose of the first topic is to allow facilitators and participants to come to a mutual (collaborative) understanding of the extent of any active substance use disorder(s) and mental health disorder(s), and to determine if they fall into the moderate to severe range (see figure 1 on page 10). According to this schema, diagnosis is dependent on how many of the criteria an individual meets (and how often). Mild substance use problems may be sufficiently addressed through screening and brief intervention (which can sometimes result in individuals returning to low-risk use), but people with moderate substance use disorders are at the highest risk of developing a more severe problem. Therefore, abstinence from substance use becomes the most reasonable goal to pursue for those with moderate or severe substance use disorders. A proper assessment will guide development of a treatment plan. The criteria for each drug class differ, but what follows is a generalized overview of substance use disorders as described in *DSM-5*. For the specific diagnostic criteria for each individual substance use disorder—that is, for each drug class (alcohol, caffeine, cannabis, hallucinogens, inhalants, opioids, sedatives, stimulants, tobacco)—refer to *DSM-5*, pages 483–589.

DSM-5 Criteria for Substance Use Disorders

Features
The essential feature of a substance use disorder is a cluster of cognitive, behavioral, and physiological symptoms indicating that the

individual continues using the substance despite significant substance-related problems. . . . [T]he diagnosis of a substance use disorder can be applied to all 10 classes included in this *[DSM-5]* chapter except caffeine. For certain classes, some symptoms are less salient, and in a few instances not all symptoms apply (e.g., withdrawal symptoms are not specified for phencyclidine use disorder, other hallucinogen use disorder, or inhalant use disorder).

An important characteristic of substance use disorders is an underlying change in brain circuits that may persist beyond detoxification, particularly in individuals with severe disorders. The behavioral effects of these brain changes may be exhibited in the repeated relapses and intense drug craving when the individuals are exposed to drug-related stimuli. These persistent drug effects may benefit from long-term approaches to treatment.

Overall, the diagnosis of a substance use disorder is based on a pathological pattern of behaviors related to use of the substance. To assist with organization, Criterion A criteria can be considered to fit within overall groupings of *impaired control, social impairment, risky use,* and *pharmacological criteria.* Impaired control over substance use is the first criteria grouping (Criteria 1–4). The individual may take the substance in larger amounts or over a longer period than was originally intended (Criterion 1). The individual may express a persistent desire to cut down or regulate substance use and may report multiple unsuccessful efforts to decrease or discontinue use (Criterion 2). The individual may spend a great deal of time obtaining the substance, using the substance, or recovering from its effects (Criterion 3). In some instances of more severe substance use disorders, virtually all of the individual's daily activities revolve around the substance. Craving (Criterion 4) is manifested by an intense desire or urge for the drug that may occur at any time but is more likely when in an environment where the drug previously was obtained or used. Craving has also been shown to involve classical conditioning and is associated with activation of specific reward structures in the brain. Craving is queried by asking if there has ever been a time when they had such strong urges to take the drug that they could not think of anything else. Current craving is often used as a treatment outcome measure because it may be a signal of impending relapse.

Social impairment is the second grouping of criteria (Criteria 5–7). Recurrent substance use may result in a failure to fulfill major role obligations at work, school, or home (Criterion 5). The individual may continue substance use despite having persistent or recurrent social or interpersonal problems caused or exacerbated by the effects of the substance (Criterion 6). Important social, occupational, or recreational activities may be given up or reduced because of substance use (Criterion 7). The individual may withdraw from family activities and hobbies in order to use the substance.

Risky use of the substance is the third grouping of criteria (Criteria 8–9). This may take the form of recurrent substance use in situations in which it is physically hazardous (Criterion 8). The individual may continue substance use despite knowledge of having a persistent or recurrent physical or psychological problem that is likely to have been caused or exacerbated by the substance (Criterion 9). The key issue in evaluating this criterion is not the existence of the problem, but rather the individual's failure to abstain from using the substance despite the difficulty it is causing.

Pharmacological criteria are the final grouping (Criteria 10 and 11). Tolerance (Criterion 10) is signaled by requiring a markedly increased dose of the substance to achieve the desired effect or a markedly reduced effect when the usual dose is consumed. The degree to which tolerance develops varies greatly across different individuals as well as across substances and may involve a variety of central nervous system effects. For example, tolerance to respiratory depression and tolerance to sedating and motor coordination may develop at different rates, depending on the substance. Tolerance may be difficult to determine by history alone, and laboratory tests may be helpful (e.g., high blood levels of the substance coupled with little evidence of intoxication suggest that tolerance is likely). Tolerance must also be distinguished from individual variability in the initial sensitivity to the effects of particular substances. For example, some first-time alcohol drinkers show very little evidence of intoxication with three or four drinks, whereas others of similar weight and drinking histories have slurred speech and incoordination.

Withdrawal (Criterion 11) is a syndrome that occurs when blood or tissue concentrations of a substance decline in an individual who had maintained prolonged heavy use of the substance. After developing withdrawal symptoms, the individual is likely to consume the substance to relieve the symptoms. Withdrawal symptoms vary greatly across the classes of substances, and separate criteria sets for withdrawal are provided for the drug classes. Marked and generally easily measured physiological signs of withdrawal are common with alcohol, opioids, and sedatives, hypnotics, and anxiolytics. Withdrawal signs and symptoms with stimulants (amphetamines and cocaine), as well as tobacco and cannabis, are often present but may be less apparent. Significant withdrawal has *not* been documented in humans after repeated use of phencyclidine, other hallucinogens, and inhalants; therefore, this criterion is not included for these substances. Neither tolerance nor withdrawal is necessary for a diagnosis of a substance use disorder. However, for most classes of substances, a past history of withdrawal is associated with a more severe clinical course (i.e., an earlier onset of a substance use disorder, higher levels of substance intake, and a greater number of substance-related problems).

Symptoms of tolerance and withdrawal occurring during appropriate medical treatment with prescribed medications (e.g., opioid analgesics, sedatives, stimulants) are specifically *not* counted when diagnosing a substance use disorder. The appearance of normal, expected pharmacological tolerance and withdrawal during the course of medical treatment has been known to lead to an erroneous diagnosis of "addiction" even when these were the only symptoms present. Individuals whose *only* symptoms are those that occur as a result of medical treatment (i.e., tolerance and withdrawal as part of medical care when the medications are taken as prescribed) should not receive a diagnosis solely on the basis of these symptoms. However, prescription medications can be used inappropriately, and a substance use disorder can be correctly diagnosed when there are other symptoms or compulsive, drug-seeking behavior.

Severity and Specifiers
Substance use disorders occur in a broad range of severity, from mild to severe, with severity based on the number of symptom criteria endorsed. As a general estimate of severity, a *mild* substance use disorder is suggested by the presence of two to three symptoms, *moderate* by

four to five symptoms, and *severe* by six or more symptoms. Changing severity across time is also reflected by reductions or increases in the frequency and/or dose of substance use, as assessed by the individual's own report, report of knowledgeable others, clinician's observations, and biological testing. The following course specifiers and descriptive features specifiers are also available for substance use disorders: "in early remission," "in sustained remission," "on maintenance therapy," and "in a controlled environment." Definitions of each are provided within respective criteria sets.

Reprinted with permission from the *Diagnostic and Statistical Manual of Mental Disorders, Fifth Edition* (Copyright ©2013). American Psychiatric Association. All Rights Reserved.

Assessment

Diagnosis should be achieved through a clinical interview that uses *DSM-5* and other assessment tools to examine substance use history and to inventory consequences related to substance use. There are assessment tools included in the facilitator guide and on its accompanying CD-ROM that can help. In fact, there are a number of screening and assessment tools that can be useful during a comprehensive behavioral health assessment.

Many treatment centers have their own intake procedures, and many therapists have assessment tools of choice. A comprehensive mental health evaluation may include use of the MMPI, ASAM criteria, and tools that measure outcomes such as the BHI-MV.

Regardless of the tools used, a thorough assessment is important at this stage because a significant number of men and women who seek treatment for a substance use disorder are suffering from a co-occurring disorder *in addition* to their substance use problem. The diagnosis of co-occurring disorders during assessment is important, as that determines whether a participant should follow treatment through the TSF program or the TSF-COD program. Concurrent treatment for co-occurring disorders is an important part of a treatment plan for someone in the TSF-COD program.

The TSF and TSF-COD programs also recommend measuring the effectiveness of the treatment program. For this task, we recommend the Alcoholics Anonymous Affiliation Scale (AAAS)[1] or the Twelve Step Affiliation and Practices Scale (TSAPS). The research conducted on Twelve Step fellowships strongly supports a relationship between *involvement* in a fellowship and recovery. That involvement has been found to correlate positively with abstinence and/or reduced substance use.[2] Such involvement includes meeting attendance, but it goes beyond that basic level of involvement.

The AAAS is a nine-item instrument that correlates AA group involvement with recovery outcomes. It can be administered by the facilitator both before TSF or TSF-COD is undertaken and again afterward in order to measure recovery outcomes gained throughout the program. To the extent that involvement with a support group increases as a result of TSF or TSF-COD program administration, we can expect a positive effect on recovery outcomes. That said, in order for efficacy to be properly gauged, we recommend that only those participants who attend a minimum of six TSF or TSF-COD sessions use the AAAS. The AAAS is in the public domain, which means it is free, and you don't need to worry about issues like copyright infringement. A copy, along with scoring instructions, can be found in each facilitator guide and on the CD-ROM that accompanies the facilitator guide.

The TSAPS is a twenty-one-item instrument that measures the extent to which the person endorses and internalizes key Twelve Step ideas and beliefs, as well as the degree to which he or she is actively practicing the Twelve Steps. As such, the TSAPS may be good for those involved in Twelve Step fellowships outside AA. Similar to AAAS, the TSAPS can be administered both before TSF or TSF-COD is undertaken, and again afterward to measure recovery outcomes gained through the course of the program. But TSAPS isn't fellowship-specific, meaning anyone involved with any Twelve Step fellowship can use the instrument. A copy of this instrument, along with scoring instructions, is also included in each facilitator guide and on the CD-ROM that accompanies the facilitator guide.

After administration of the assessment tools, results are discussed with participants. In cases where participants meet the criteria for a moderate to severe substance use disorder, the discussion should move into understanding the problem. This involves examining how a participant's lifestyle has been affected by substance use.

There may be situations where "compliant" participants (who merely seek to placate the facilitator) may very well agree to a diagnosis without truly accepting it. A false commitment to participate (which the participant does not follow through on) may result from external pressure to pursue abstinence and get involved with a Twelve Step fellowship, so it is important to focus primarily on the consequences of use and leave the discussion of possible solutions until facilitation of Core Topic 2: Acceptance. The participant may not see some of the problems he or she is experiencing as consequences of substance use. As a result, it can be helpful to discuss problems the participant is experiencing as part of the diagnostic assessment and point out later that these are actually consequences of substance use.

Consequences

Consequences of alcohol and other drug use can be divided into several categories, and it is recommended that those categories be worked into the discussion through conversation, not by reading through the list. The list is extensive, and not every item or category will apply to individual participants. Additionally, there may be consequences not listed on pages 72–74 that the participant discloses. The facilitator can take notes during this discussion so that the consequences he or she identifies can be discussed again later, when the participant is further along in the program.

Additional consequences will emerge in the course of treatment. For example, youths are more likely to engage in indiscriminate drug use in party situations, which can lead to aggression, sexual assault, or overdose. However, they might not admit to this during the assessment. Similarly, "pre-drinking" or "pre-using" (drinking or getting high prior to a party) can be thought of as a consequence for young people because a party involving substance use may involve using beforehand as well, which can result in being under the influence before even going to the social event. Again, this might not be discussed in the initial assessment. Still other individuals may not initially admit to experiencing blackouts, but will do so later on. And so on.

Physical Consequences

- hypertension (high blood pressure)
- diabetes
- gastrointestinal (digestive) problems
- sleep problems: insomnia, unrestful sleep, early waking
- auto, home, or job accidents or injuries
- emergency room visits
- blackouts
- overdose
- passing out
- heart problems
- liver disease

Legal Consequences

- driving under the influence (DUI) arrests
- arrests for disorderly conduct or assault
- arrests for possession of illegal substances
- problems encountered in the military related to alcohol and/or other drugs (veterans only)
- illegal activities for which the participant was not caught (e.g., driving under the influence)

Social Consequences

- occupational problems, such as excessive sick leave; poor, declining, or uneven performance evaluations; being fired; being forced to undergo assessment and/or treatment
- school problems such as declining or failing grades, increased absenteeism, or behavioral issues
- indiscriminate use of drugs (for example, taking unknown drugs at a party)

- "pre-drinking" or "pre-using," meaning drinking or using drugs intentionally in advance of a social function
- significant-other problems, such as chronic conflicts over drinking or using; conflicts over money spent on alcohol or other drugs; conflicts over deceit, unreliability, infidelity, or abuse; breakdown of communication and intimacy
- conflicts with children or relatives over use
- problems functioning effectively as a parent
- loss of old friends as a result of alcohol or other drug use
- isolating oneself from others

Sexual Consequences

- problems of arousal (impotence in men, painful intercourse in women)
- loss of sexual desire
- sexual behavior that the participant would not choose to engage in if sober (frequenting strip clubs, "massage parlors," or prostitutes; having sex with strangers; and so on)
- sexual victimization or exploitation (rape, prostitution, pornography)

Psychological Consequences

- irritability or moodiness
- depression
- suicidal thoughts
- loss of motivation, drive, or interest
- memory problems (especially "forgetfulness")
- disorientation
- impulsivity
- aggressiveness
- confused thinking
- hallucinations

Financial Consequences

- creditor problems, such as overextended credit, revoked credit cards
- mortgage or rent problems
- delinquent loans
- problems "making ends meet" due to money spent on alcohol and other drugs
- fines
- legal fees associated with alcohol- or other drug-related arrests

This topic includes a summarization of the severity of a substance use disorder using *DSM-5* criteria and the consequences that support that diagnosis. It then introduces the *TSF* program. If co-occurring disorders have been identified, these should be discussed, and concurrent treatment should be included as part of the TSF-COD treatment plan. The preferred outcome of the assessment is to have the participant and facilitator reach a consensus on diagnosis. However, the facilitator needs to be prepared to "agree to disagree" at this point on the matter of diagnosis. In either case, facilitation should flow into Core Topic 2: Acceptance.

Recovery Tasks

All TSF sessions end with the facilitator suggesting some activities for the participant to engage in before the next session. These suggested activities are referred to as recovery tasks and are part of active treatment. They are followed up on at the start of each new TSF session. At the end of Core Topic 1: Assessment, there are two suggested recovery tasks. The first is to read through the Core Topic 1: Assessment section of the participant workbook. The second is for the participant to attend one or more Twelve Step fellowship meetings and record their experiences in the workbook. A participant may be provided a published list of local meetings, or the facilitator and participant may go online together to identify convenient meetings. For those in the TSF-COD program, a third recovery task involves reaching out to a mental health professional to discuss the participant's mental health diagnosis and treatment plan.

Research shows that men and women who consistently attended at least sixty Twelve Step fellowship meetings per year following treatment had a 79 percent chance of remaining abstinent five years later. In contrast, those who attended Twelve Step meetings for only the first year after treatment had about a 40 percent chance of remaining abstinent after five years.[3] Data like this can be helpful when discussing recovery tasks.

■ ■ ■

7

Core Topic 2: Acceptance

DIMENSION	KEY CONCEPT	CORE PROCESS	MARKERS
Social/ Behavioral	Getting active	Building a support network	• Active participation • Sponsor • Home group
Cognitive	Denial	Acceptance and surrender	• Identifying as a recovering person • Acceptance of abstinence as a personal goal
Spiritual	Personal growth	Spiritual awakening	• Moral inventory • Prayer/meditation • Altruism • Spiritual activities

Following assessment, the TSF program examines a participant's willingness to see a connection—"connect the dots"—between his or her substance use and negative consequences. The program also explores whether the participant has ever attempted to control or stop substance use before, and the participant and facilitator discuss those attempts. This discussion continues the one about consequences that began in Core Topic 1: Assessment.

At heart, Core Topic 2: Acceptance is about exploring Step One of the Twelve Steps and seeing how well a participant can identify with it. The First Step represents a major cognitive leap from *denial* ("I don't have a problem") to *acceptance* ("Alcohol or drug use has caused me serious problems").

We admitted that we were powerless over our addiction, that our lives had become unmanageable.[1]

Denial

More generally, denial refers to the emotional and intellectual difficulties resulting from personal limitation or loss. With addiction, denial involves difficulty facing and accepting the loss of one's control over substance use, as well as the need to give up using for good.

> Most of us have been unwilling to admit we were real alcoholics. No person likes to think he is bodily and mentally different from his fellows. Therefore, it is not surprising that our drinking careers have been characterized by countless vain attempts to prove we could drink like other people.
>
> —*Alcoholics Anonymous*[2]

> Denial of our addiction kept us sick, but our honest admission of addiction enabled us to stop using.
>
> —*Narcotics Anonymous*[3]

Limitation and loss cause pain, and it is normal for people to try to protect themselves from pain. One of the easiest ways to protect oneself is to deny the reality of the limitation or loss. Limitation and loss arouse feelings of anxiety, anger, shame, sadness, inadequacy, and/or guilt. They pose a decided threat to self-esteem. Any or all of these factors can motivate an individual to avoid—deny—coming to terms with or accepting a personal limitation such as addiction.

One way to approach denial is to describe it as a normal part of the grief process. People seem to be naturally disposed to deny their losses and limitations, and a substance use disorder confronts us with just such a loss and limitation. Recovery means not only "losing" the mood-altering substances upon which participants have come to depend but also very possibly "losing" a social network and a lifestyle that supported addiction.

Another way to approach denial is to think of it as "bargaining." Considering Step One and the acceptance process, bargaining can be seen through the participant's belief that he or she can "safely" drink or use and is "in control" of substance use. Core Topic 1: Assessment presented evidence that contradicted that belief. By bargaining, a participant is unsuccessfully trying to control use. And by refusing to accept loss of control, the participant is denying reality.

Bargaining and denial become most evident when participants "tempt fate" by using once or twice between sessions. Participants may be trying to convince themselves that they are still in control. It's important to look at Step One and ask what role denial might play in the refusal to give up substance use altogether. After Core Topic 1: Assessment, continued use between sessions doesn't support a participant's ability to control use; it reiterates his or her inability to stop. Bargaining may have played a role in previous attempts to quit or cut down, preventing progression toward acceptance.

Though denial is natural, it is dangerous for someone with a severe substance use disorder who refuses to admit his or her loss of control. Addiction is a biopsychosocial disorder where denial can cause people to get sicker, and that can be fatal.

Slips and Relapses

There are some who argue that there are no such things as "slips," only "relapses." However, it is worth distinguishing between a person who has made progress in sustaining sobriety (for example, an increased number of sober days and decreased amount of use) and a person who has returned to and/or remained at pre-treatment levels of use. In the instance of the former, this participant's use between sober periods can be called a slip.

When a participant has a slip, the first goal is to analyze the slip. Understand where the participant *was*, what the participant was *feeling*, and what the participant was *thinking* when the slip occurred. Slips are common in early recovery in situations conducive to use, but a participant will need to create alternate scenarios—situations that support recovery rather than substance use. Alternate scenarios should address all three aspects of a slip or relapse: the *situation*, the *emotions*, and the *thoughts* associated with drinking or using. Some examples include calling a hotline, contacting a sponsor or fellowship member, going to a meeting, meditating, and engaging in another activity.

Risk is higher in social networks and/or at events that support substance use (tailgating, sports bars, and so on). Men and women with moderate to severe substance use disorders often have social networks that support substance use. Acceptance involves finding social networks and events that support sobriety—something that can take time. While undertaking the process of change, a slip may occur.

Emotions such as anger, depression, loneliness, boredom, ennui, and anxiety often result in urges to drink or use, but positive emotional states like excitement and joy can cause people to use as well. Part of recovery involves being able to identify risky thoughts, emotions, and situations and avoid them when possible. Entertaining even a fleeting thought such as "one drink" or "one hit" can easily be a prelude to a slip, if not a full-blown relapse—especially for someone diagnosed with a severe substance use disorder. Recovery may include slips along the way, but it is important to use them as learning opportunities. Discussing the location, feelings, and thoughts that occurred at the time of a slip will help participants identify alternative scenarios to seek out in the future—ones that support sobriety.

Negative thoughts (self-statements) following a slip can lead to a full-blown relapse. Examples include "I slipped up; I'm a failure; I give up" and "This is too hard; I can't do it." Twelve Step fellowships recognize that recovery is a bumpy road and can provide support after a slip. It can be very useful for participants to articulate short-term thoughts while continuing to focus on the long-term goal of abstinence. Indeed, most worthwhile goals in life are not achieved without some failure and frustration along the way.

Acceptance

Common human reactions to the idea that personal willpower is not sufficient to conquer substance use can range from anxiety to depression to anger. In fact, it is rare that we humans will accept a personal limitation—especially one of this magnitude—with poise. The Serenity Prayer *reminds us to try.*

We live in a culture where social drinking and social drug use is a norm for a large portion of the population. Genuine acceptance often comes gradually as a result, frequently accompanied by considerable emotionality and much defensiveness. People employ all sorts of defenses against facing limitations of personal willpower: "I don't have a problem," "I'm not so bad," "I could do it by myself if I really set my mind to it," and so on.

Step One has a reputation for being the most difficult. It may take time, and that may require focusing on Core Topic 2: Acceptance for more than one session. It may be helpful to explore other topics and return for another session on Core Topic 2: Acceptance later in a participant's treatment plan. For some, the acceptance process might involve exploring the other Twelve Steps holistically before genuine acceptance is achieved. Keep in mind that there are two other dimensions of recovery. Many participants, for example, report that they only took Step One seriously after attending many meetings, having some slips, and making lifestyle changes supportive of abstinence. Regardless of how a participant reaches acceptance, it is fundamental to the TSF program and is necessary for successful recovery.

Acceptance can be thought of as a process that a participant goes through. The acceptance process starts with a participant accepting that he or she has a problem with substance use, moves on to accepting that substance use is gradually making life more difficult and is causing more and more problems, and ends with accepting that substance use is not able to be effectively limited, and the only alternative is to give it up.

It is powerlessness—to either stop or effectively control use—that defines addiction. It is not always helpful to present that information in direct terms to someone with a severe substance use disorder, at least not initially. Recovery requires that these men and women must ultimately accept failure of personal willpower—despite their best efforts or good intentions—and face the increasing unmanageability that substance use is creating. Teens are notorious for believing in their immortality, and they can require patience in discussing Step One. Persistence in pointing out the objective consequences associated with their substance use (poor school attendance, failing grades, loss of former friends, abandonment of former activities, indiscriminate sex, and so on) will most often prevail, even with teens.

Participants may be encouraged to find additional counseling to coincide with active participation in a Twelve Step fellowship. According to the *Alcoholics Anonymous 2014 Membership Survey*, fully 58 percent of respondents stated that they pursued some form of personal counseling (psychological, spiritual, etc.) after starting to go to AA or NA.[4] Counseling may be a good setting for exploring personal issues (abuse, abandonment, failed attachments, and so on) that may have influenced a participant's substance use. In fact, substance use may have suppressed thoughts and emotions related to those issues. Additional counseling can help participants address relevant issues in a timeframe and setting that feels safe.

Bob: Taking the First Step

Bob and Kathy had been married for twenty years. They went to see a counselor, ostensibly for marital counseling. Though initially obscured by discussions and arguments about money, children, and sex, it became apparent after a while that Bob had a significant drinking problem that needed to be evaluated. He was asked to come in individually for two sessions to talk about this.

It turned out that Bob showed several signs of a severe alcohol use disorder. He had a powerful tolerance, drank daily, and had experienced a number of drinking-related negative consequences—not the least of which was his seriously strained marriage. In addition, he was in trouble at work as a result of declining productivity—another negative consequence of his drinking, but one he'd so far kept from his wife.

At first, Bob was reluctant to shift the focus of therapy from his troubled marriage to his drinking. The therapist assured him that his concerns about his marriage were legitimate and would be dealt with; first, however, Bob needed to do something about his drinking or risk losing his job and possibly his marriage.

Bob's private struggle to control his alcohol consumption is a testament to stubborn determination as much as it is a classic story about the power of addiction. Having started drinking as a youth barely twelve years old by sipping beers he stole from the refrigerator, Bob had been drinking continuously for thirty years. Bob said things didn't get bad until after he was married and the kids were born. Two things happened then. First, he felt obligated to stay in a job that paid well but that he had previously intended to leave. Second, his relationship with Kathy had, in his words, "become diluted" by the demands of family life.

It was around this time—after his youngest child, a daughter, was born—that Bob developed the habit of having "a cocktail or two" every night after work, before dinner. For a long time, Kathy went along with this, though she noticed that "a cocktail or two" eventually became three, four, or more. She didn't much care for alcohol herself and had little personal experience with drinking problems in her own family. Therefore, she was inclined to tolerate these gradual changes in her husband's drinking behavior.

As time went on, Bob began to exhibit signs of an alcohol use disorder. Instead of eating in the company cafeteria, Bob found himself going to a nearby pub for lunch two or three times a week. He'd have a couple of cocktails every time. By the time he got home, he was anxious to "relax"—his euphemism for having more cocktails.

Kathy and the kids soon found that anything that stood between Bob and his cocktails made him irritable. He didn't want to be bothered with their problems until he was "relaxed." Of course, by the time he was "relaxed," Bob was also intoxicated. That made him emotionally unstable and prone to being irritable. So the rest of the family learned to avoid him. Kathy took to solving most of the household problems by herself, or else she let them go. The kids, meanwhile, led their own lives and had minimal communication with their father. At that point, Bob's drinking had become a concern for Kathy, though she didn't know how best to approach the subject with him.

Bob tried to avoid coming to terms with his loss of control over drinking—as fiercely as any alcoholic might. His first line of defense was to get angry whenever anyone, such as his wife or his children, brought up the subject. After blowing up, he'd usually change the subject and launch into an attack on the other person, or he'd complain long and loudly about some other problem, like finances or his annoying in-laws. In response to the ever-growing list of household maintenance chores that were going undone, he pleaded fatigue. After all, he said, he worked hard all week and needed the weekends to unwind.

Not surprisingly, Bob's denial extended beyond his outward behavior. His denial even went inward, to his own thought processes. He went out of his way to associate with men who drank as much as or more than he did and then comforted himself by comparing the level of his own use to theirs. He concluded that his drinking was merely "average" (and therefore "normal") among his peers. At times when he felt guilty pouring himself that fifth or sixth martini, he'd tell himself that he deserved it—because of the stress of having to endure an unsatisfying job. He wrote off his troubles at work to a combination of bad luck and a vindictive boss, and his increasing tendency toward sexual impotence he attributed to his wife's rejection of him and her preoccupation with the children.

In these and other ways, Bob was able to fend off the complaints of others, as well as his own nagging conscience. Meanwhile, the quality of his life and his own health steadily declined. Though he was very hesitant to admit it, privately Bob had been struggling unsuccessfully to control his drinking for a long time. He hadn't wanted to be like his own father—a man Bob described as a "quiet drunk," whose drinking was less visible than Bob's but no less problematic. Bob explained that his father's drinking caused him to be socially isolated and a "nonfactor" within his family growing up.

Bob used various methods to try to control his drinking: drinking only wine, drinking only beer (no cocktails) at lunch, drinking from a smaller glass, adding more ice cubes to his cocktails, and so on. All the while, he was conscious on some level that he was gradually losing control, yet he continued to convince himself that he was really all right. It wasn't until he was caught with liquor on his breath at work that Bob's shell of self-deceit finally and abruptly shattered. For Bob, recovery began when he told this story to the therapist and subsequently to Kathy.

It was only when his therapist helped him to "connect the dots" between his drinking and disciplinary action at work, his deteriorating marriage and family life, and even his doctor's warning about early symptoms of diabetes, that Bob reluctantly took a hard look at his drinking and his inability to control it. It marked Bob's acceptance of his limitations when it came to alcohol.

Recovery Tasks

An agreement should be reached between the facilitator and the participants on how many and which Twelve Step fellowship meetings participants will attend before the next session. Additionally, participants are encouraged to continue reading conference-approved Twelve Step fellowship literature, such as *Alcoholics Anonymous, Narcotics Anonymous, Twelve Steps and Twelve Traditions,* and other readings recommended by the facilitator. The participant workbooks help with reviewing content, tracking sober days, and analyzing slips.

■ ■ ■

8

Core Topic 3: Surrender

DIMENSION	KEY CONCEPT	CORE PROCESS	MARKERS
Social/ Behavioral	Getting active	Building a support network	• Active participation • Sponsor • Home group
Cognitive	Denial	Acceptance and surrender	• Identifying as a recovering person • Acceptance of abstinence as a personal goal
Spiritual	Personal growth	Spiritual awakening	• Moral inventory • Prayer/meditation • Altruism • Spiritual activities

Core Topic 3: Surrender examines a participant's willingness to reach out beyond himself or herself and follow the Twelve Step program. This involves trusting in a power greater than individual willpower to support sustained sobriety. Surrender and acceptance are core processes in cognitive change, and Core Topic 3: Surrender introduces personal growth by discussing Higher Powers and encouraging active involvement in Twelve Step fellowships. This topic picks up where Core Topic 2: Acceptance left off.

While also examining psychotherapy and medication-assisted therapy, Core Topic 3: Surrender focuses largely on Step Two and Step Three of the Twelve Steps. Fellowship involvement and meeting attendance—social/behavioral change—are central to the process of surrender. Fellowship offers support and hope through success stories of other fellowship members. It plays an important role in the change processes within both the cognitive and the spiritual recovery dimensions as well. And fellowships may also be able to provide additional resources to help with Step Two and Step Three:

> We came to believe that a Power greater than ourselves could restore us to sanity.

> We made a decision to turn our will and our lives over to the care of God *as we understood Him.*[1]

Surrender

Whereas Step One involves "accepting the problem," Step Two and Step Three involve "surrendering to the solution." Acceptance and surrender are understood as part of a cognitive change process because few people in recovery claim to have been able to move from acceptance to surrender in one quick leap. As a result, the topic of surrender may need to be covered in more than one session, and the structure and flexibility of the TSF program will easily accommodate this.

Step One represents the first milestone in recovery: a willingness to stop denying a connection between substance use and its consequences. There is a sense of loss associated with Step One, but Step Two represents hope: a willingness to reach out beyond personal willpower for a solution. This is the second milestone of recovery. The third milestone, Step Three, challenges the individual to take action. It serves to move one further away from helplessness and toward hope and support. Together, the first three Steps form the foundation for recovery.

Taken together, Steps One, Two, and Three can also be conceptualized as constituting an epiphany, which is commonly defined as a moment in which a person suddenly sees or understands something in a new and very clear way. Epiphanies are often associated with major life changes, such as Joan of Arc's famous and sudden realization while gardening that her true purpose in life was to free France. Others' epiphanies may be less dramatic, but they are nevertheless life changing. And that is exactly what recovering people experience once they are able to truly embrace these first three Steps.

Although the word *God* is included in Step Three, the phrase *as we understood Him* leaves this Step open to different interpretations and beliefs. Indeed, Bill Wilson was a lifelong agnostic. During work on Step Two, fellowships themselves often represent "a Power greater than ourselves" for many people in recovery. For them, the success stories in peer fellowship are a testament to its "higher power." The following are excerpts that describe the process of surrender.

> The great fact is just this, and nothing less: That we have had deep and effective spiritual experiences which have revolutionized our whole attitude toward life, toward our fellows and toward God's universe. The central fact of our lives today is the absolute certainty that our Creator has entered into our hearts and lives in a way which is indeed miraculous. He has commenced to accomplish those things for us which we could never do by ourselves.
>
> —*Alcoholics Anonymous* [2]

> You can, if you wish, make A.A. itself your "higher power." Here's a very large group of people who have solved their alcohol problem. In this respect they are certainly a power greater than you. . . . Surely you can have faith in them.
>
> —*Twelve Steps and Twelve Traditions* [3]

Discussing Higher Powers

Twelve Step fellowships are sometimes mistaken for being "religious organizations" that pressure their members to pledge belief in a Judeo-Christian God. This is not true. Religions are governed by a written dogma that is administered by designated clergy and supervised by a clerical hierarchy. Twelve Step fellowships have none of these things, and it is important to reassure participants of this.

There is no central body within Twelve Step fellowships that dictates the content of meetings, or what Higher Power members should ascribe to. The sole requirement for membership in a Twelve Step fellowship is a desire to stop substance use. Newcomers who find themselves in a meeting where they are uncomfortable should be encouraged to "shop around" for meetings that they feel more comfortable in.

Twelve Step fellowships are intentionally open to people with a wide range of personal religious beliefs. The diversity of fellowships makes it possible to find meetings that attract a wide variety of men and women. So while it is certainly possible to find meetings for members with strong Christian beliefs, it is also possible to find meetings for agnostics and atheists. This is especially true in urban areas. These meetings all share a belief in a "power" greater than the personal willpower that proved ineffective in stopping or controlling substance use.

> First, Alcoholics Anonymous does not demand that you believe anything. All of its Twelve Steps are but suggestions. Second, to get sober and to stay sober, you don't have to swallow all of Step Two right now. Looking back, I find that I took it piecemeal myself. Third, all you really need is a truly open mind. Just resign from the debating society and quit bothering yourself with such deep questions as whether it was the hen or the egg that came first. Again I say, all you need is the open mind.
>
> —*Twelve Steps and Twelve Traditions*[4]

Naturally, when facilitating a dialogue about Higher Powers, it is important that the facilitator keep an open mind. Personal religious preferences on the part of the facilitator should not influence facilitation of the TSF program, else the participant may react negatively to the facilitator's personal beliefs. The concept of surrender should be rooted simply and firmly in the understanding that personal willpower alone is not sufficient to overcome addiction. How the power in Step Two and Step Three is understood is up to individual participants, and facilitators should respect those beliefs.

> Lack of power, that was our dilemma. We had to find a power by which we could live, and it had to be a *Power greater than ourselves*. Obviously. But where and how were we to find this Power?
>
> Well, that's exactly what this book is about. Its main object is to enable you to find a Power greater than yourself which will solve your problem. That means we have

written a book which we believe to be spiritual as well as
moral.

—*Alcoholics Anonymous*[5]

Medication-Assisted Treatment

Individual surrender involves deciding to abandon personal willpower
as a solution to a substance use disorder and deciding to reach out
instead. Involvement in a Twelve Step fellowship is a foundational part
of recovery, offering a pathway to a new lifestyle and a spiritual awakening that can assist with recovery. However, that involvement does not
need to be the sole basis for recovery.

Concurrent psychotherapy and Twelve Step fellowship involvement
can be powerful, and indeed that approach is encouraged—as long as
psychotherapy supports Twelve Step fellowship involvement. For some,
concurrent psychotherapy can help to address underlying issues that
may have been influencing substance use, such as trauma, abandonment, or abuse. In fact, both TSF and TSF-COD are examples of psychotherapy-assisted recovery.

During the process of surrender, an individual may find himself
or herself opening up to a variety of support—from a psychologist or
psychiatrist, from a sponsor, from a pastor or rabbi, from fellowship
members, and so on. As a participant works through Step Two and
Step Three and discovers his or her own path to recovery, additional
avenues of support can improve recovery outcomes. But additional
support should always occur in tandem with Twelve Step fellowship
involvement.

Some participants may choose to participate in medication-assisted
treatment. The very process of surrender may be what makes some participants more comfortable with medication-assisted treatment. This
can create conflict with those who view recovery as requiring complete
abstinence from all drugs. However, recovery from any health condition can sometimes require medication, and a substance use disorder
is no different. There are a variety of reasons for prescribing medication during treatment, from mental health reasons to controlling
physical withdrawal symptoms. Ultimately, the choice to participate in
medication-assisted treatment should be made by the participant—with

input from his or her doctor, therapist, or Higher Power. Participants taking part in medication-assisted treatment are encouraged to find Twelve Step fellowship groups that support this approach.

> No A.A. member should "play doctor"; all medical advice and treatment should come from a qualified physician. . . .
>
> . . . Just as it is wrong to enable or support any alcoholic to become re-addicted to any drug, it's equally wrong to deprive any alcoholic of medication, which can alleviate or control other disabling physical and/or emotional problems.
>
> —*The A.A. Member—Medications and Other Drugs*[6]

> God has abundantly supplied this world with fine doctors, psychologists, and practitioners of various kinds. Do not hesitate to take your health problems to such persons. Most of them give freely of themselves, that their fellows may enjoy sound minds and bodies. Try to remember that though God has wrought miracles among us, we should never belittle a good doctor or psychiatrist. Their services are often indispensable in treating a newcomer and in following his case afterward.
>
> —*Alcoholics Anonymous*[7]

> Some members recover in NA with mental illness that requires medication. Just as we wouldn't suggest that an insulin-dependent diabetic addict stop taking their insulin, we don't tell mentally ill addicts to stop taking their prescribed medication. We leave medical issues up to doctors.
>
> —*In Times of Illness*[8]

Twelve Step fellowships have a long and rich oral tradition. The telling of personal stories of loss and recovery is a powerful way to share the lessons learned in AA and NA. Reading about others' experiences with addiction is also important. Stories like Maria's can be powerful in delivery of the TSF program.

Maria: Struggling to Surrender

Maria had an addiction to both alcohol and cocaine and was under-achieving in virtually every aspect of her life. Maria was typical of women and men who have suffered abuse—she balked when she was confronted with Step Two and Step Three. Her distrust and cynicism stood in the way of finding hope for herself, of finding a Higher Power in whom she could have faith, and of finding support. The roots of her distrust are not hard to understand. Abandoned by her natural father through divorce, she was later sexually abused by a stepfather over a period of years. Her mother divorced the stepfather when the abuse was discovered, but Maria's relationship with her mother was badly strained as well by then. When Maria was fifteen, the one sibling with whom she felt close, an older sister, was killed in a car accident. It is little wonder that Maria had difficulty accepting the concept of a loving Higher Power—much less turning her life and will over to that power.

As a lesbian, Maria was comfortable with her sexual orientation, but she was decidedly uncomfortable around men. Her previous partners seemed to be more dependent on her than she was on them, and they were inclined to hold her in awe. Indeed, Maria was an attractive, intelligent, and talented woman.

Despite her intelligence and sophistication, Maria was naive in many ways. Her façade of bravado covered up deep insecurities and severe substance use disorders. At her mother's urging, she sought psychotherapy after another long string of emergency room detoxifications. There, she was told frankly by an attending physician that her best (and perhaps only) hope was to get to a Twelve Step meeting immediately and to go to as many as necessary in order to stay sober, one day at a time.

Maria had tried AA and NA before, and each time she'd had a mixed reaction. On the one hand, she liked the warm feeling of acceptance she got at meetings. On the other hand, some things were problematic for her. It turned her off that men would sometimes approach her in a way that made her uncomfortable. "They would ask me to go for coffee," she said, "but all the time they were looking me up and down." This upset Maria and made her angry.

To complicate matters, she had a self-destructive tendency to accommodate the men despite her own anger, no doubt connected in some way to her childhood abuse. Having coffee and talking with a man she didn't want to be with made her feel trapped. This was especially likely to happen with outwardly appropriate men whose personal intentions she had reason to suspect. If she saw a man a second time, at another meeting, and he approached her again, she would slip out the back door and never return.

Maria returned to her psychotherapist (who had also recommended Twelve Step fellowships). She told the therapist that she was sober so far through the support of AA and NA, explaining that the hardest Step for her had not been admitting powerlessness. "No," she said, "Step One was easy for me. By then, I was ready to admit defeat. It was the solution I couldn't bring myself to swallow."

Maria solved this problem through a combination of assertiveness and networking. She worked with her therapist on learning to say no, politely but firmly, to invitations she was not interested in accepting. That way she could eventually go to mixed meetings and not feel anxious. Next, she found a couple of women's meetings and started going to them. There she talked not only about her addiction but also about her discomfort at the other meetings. She was encouraged to find a sponsor she could trust and to use the sponsor as a source of advice and support in both matters. She did. "I found a beautiful, wise, and kind woman old enough to be my mother," she laughed. This woman helped her, over time, to break her self-destructive pattern and pushed her toward betterment by setting appropriate expectations for her.

But Maria was also bothered about the position Twelve Step fellowships had on God. All she heard, it seemed, was people talking about God. This made her almost as uncomfortable as the men who came on to her, since she had nothing positive to say about either God or religion. She could not bring herself to believe in a God that she regarded as "a sexist, vindictive male image—a way for men to worship themselves."

One day she was sitting in a meeting trying hard to overcome the desire to get drunk that had been nagging her all day. After a speaker finished talking on the subject of "Odd, or God?" an old man who had been sitting quietly next to her grunted aloud and shifted in his seat. "Well," he said quietly, addressing no one in particular, "speaking just for me, AA has nothing much at all to do with God. It has to do with staying sober, pure and simple. I get tired sometimes of listening to too much God-talk. It makes me shiver. AA is a place where I can go and be with sober people. It's been that way for me for twenty-eight years. If you want to stay sober, go to meetings. If that's not enough, then you live at meetings, like I did for about a year when I first got sober."

Maria found herself moved by the simple honesty of his remarks, and she was touched when the rest of the group simply thanked the old man for sharing his thoughts. Then someone else spoke, and the meeting moved on. "That was it," said Maria. "No arguing. No recriminations. That old guy just said out loud that he thought God was unnecessary, and no one argued with him! No one kicked him out! That's when I realized that if AA could be a home for him, it could be one for me too."

For Maria, the Higher Power she could believe in turned out to be the fellowship itself, and in particular the women's and LGBT meetings she preferred to attend. For her, the fellowship resonated with her through its support and kindness; its ability to accept diversity, fault, and failure with love; its encouragement of honesty; and its collective wisdom. She had always felt different, alienated, and used, and she wanted more than anything to be accepted and respected. AA and NA gave her that, and her groups were all the Higher Power she needed to stay sober. "It's all about the love," she explained.

Recovery Tasks

As part of this topic, the facilitator and participants decide which Twelve Step fellowship meetings participants are willing to attend before the next session. Participants are encouraged to attend different kinds of meetings, such as Step meetings and discussion meetings. Additionally, participants are encouraged to socialize before and after meetings and network with other fellowship members. Asking for a temporary sponsor is a good idea. Role-playing is recommended for socially anxious or socially unskilled participants. Continued reading of conference-approved Twelve Step fellowship literature is also recommended. The participant workbooks help with reviewing content, tracking sober days, and analyzing slips.

■ ■ ■

9

Core Topic 4: Getting Active in Twelve Step Fellowships

DIMENSION	KEY CONCEPT	CORE PROCESS	MARKERS
Social/ Behavioral	Getting active	Building a support network	• Active participation • Sponsor • Home group
Cognitive	Denial	Acceptance and surrender	• Identifying as a recovering person • Acceptance of abstinence as a personal goal
Spiritual	Personal growth	Spiritual awakening	• Moral inventory • Prayer/meditation • Altruism • Spiritual activities

Core Topic 4: Getting Active in Twelve Step Fellowships delves into the social/behavioral dimension. "Getting active" refers to the idea that recovery comes only through "working the program" (which includes attending meetings, involvement in a Twelve Step fellowship, networking, and sponsorship). Getting active is helpful for support through all Twelve Steps. For newcomers, getting active provides critical support through the tough, early days and weeks of recovery, as they digest and react to Steps One, Two, and Three. Fellowship offers ongoing support to members as they progress through all Twelve Steps. For those who have been in recovery for a while, becoming a sponsor is an important part of Step Twelve. Material covered in this topic includes an examination of the many ways in which substance use disorders progressively affect a person's lifestyle (including habits, social networks, and ways of thinking) and the changes necessary for building a resilient recovery. Believing in the Twelve Steps is not enough. Recovery requires action—it means getting involved and committing to making recovery a priority.

> You might be on the right track, but you'll still get run over if you just sit there.
>
> —Will Rogers

Getting Active

In combination with Steps One, Two, and Three, getting active predates and is consistent with the theory at the heart of cognitive-behavioral treatment approaches.

> Just stopping drinking is not enough. Just *not drinking* is a negative, sterile thing. That is clearly demonstrated by our experience. To *stay* stopped, we've found we need to put in place of the drinking a positive program of action.
>
> —*Living Sober*[1]

This paradigm for understanding the change process from a cognitive-behavioral perspective is most closely associated with the work of psychologist Albert Ellis. His theory holds that an individual's thoughts influence both emotions and behaviors—in other words, emotions and behaviors follow thoughts.[2] Cognitive-behavioral therapy approaches seek to change thought patterns in order to affect behavioral and emotional change. For example, a participant may be assisted in shifting her thinking from "This is too hard; I can't do it" to "This is a challenge, but I am up to it." A change like that can make the difference between success and failure. Similarly, a man might resent a family member—an emotion that can invite substance use. However, helping this man to think "Live and let live" or "Let go and let God" can help to minimize resentment and its risks.

Some individuals in recovery claim that they became active in a fellowship as a means of staying sober long before they accepted the idea that they were unable to control their use, even when substance use was making their lives unmanageable. In other words, behavioral change came before cognitive change. Though this may be true for some, the more common pathway to recovery begins with cognitive change and progresses to action.

Getting active refers to the behavioral and social changes that participants need to make in order to support their recovery. Much of this involves lifestyle changes, such as habits, activities, and interests, along with shifts in one's social network away from one that supports substance use and toward one supportive of sobriety. An individual with a moderate or severe substance use disorder needs to stop and think before systematically and purposefully replacing old habits, relationships, and ways of thinking. Considering the scope of change that sustained recovery requires, it is little wonder that many participants become highly resistant to TSF facilitation at this stage, particularly in following through with suggested recovery tasks. The facilitator should be prepared for this. After all, getting active means committing to major changes.

Attending Meetings

Establishing a new network of friends will be critical to a participant's recovery, and starting to attend meetings marks the beginning of that process. But merely going to meetings is not the same as "working the program." Passive attendance at meetings is not likely to help a participant when he or she experiences strong urges or after he or she experiences a slip. At those times, a participant needs to know what to do—whom to call and where to go—and he or she needs to feel comfortable taking action without hesitation.

Meetings can follow a variety of formats—speaker meetings, Step meetings, discussion meetings, women's and men's meetings, and so on. Since Twelve Step fellowships do not exert any centralized control over their meetings, the variety of meeting types has proliferated over time.

Participants may need help selecting meetings that seem most appropriate for them. Some participants may be comfortable going to closed meetings right away, but others may prefer open meetings to ease into the program. The skeptical, ambivalent, or shy newcomer should be encouraged to simply "go and listen" at a few different meetings. A participant's comfort in a meeting environment is vital, especially as he or she searches for a home meeting group. In passing along recommendations to a participant, some knowledge of the different types of meetings available locally can be helpful. Eventually, a sponsor and other fellowship friends can provide further meeting recommendations.

The question of just how many meetings participants should attend in order to achieve a positive outcome is bound to come up. Those experienced with Twelve Step fellowship might say "as many as necessary." A 2014 survey of AA members indicated an average attendance of 2.5 meetings per week.[3] However, research conducted over the past several decades has yielded some relevant and valuable insights on this question.

One sixteen-year study included three groups of individuals prior to entering treatment for alcohol use disorders: those who chose to attend AA meetings but did not enter formal treatment, those who sought treatment but didn't attend AA meetings, and those who sought treatment while also attending AA meetings. The results found that those who sought treatment while also attending AA meetings were more likely to stay sober and participated in the fellowship more frequently and for a longer duration.[4]

Another study found that about two-thirds of those who attended an average of sixty AA meetings in the first year post-treatment (described as having "medium involvement") were abstinent at the one-year mark. If that same level of involvement was maintained over five years, the abstinence rate increased to nearly 80 percent.[5]

A third study followed men and women with health insurance who sought treatment through a variety of pathways (referral by primary care physician, employee assistance programs, or their own initiative). All were asked to attend at least one Twelve Step meeting a week while they were in treatment. After that, their involvement was voluntary. Results showed that Twelve Step fellowship involvement correlated with abstinence—specifically, higher attendance rates predicted higher abstinence rates fully five years following treatment.[6] Additional research has yielded similar findings.

Networking

Prior to our digital era, networking was largely limited to the phone and face-to-face meetings (often over coffee). But with smartphones, the Internet, email, instant messaging, and video chat, the idea of networking has changed, to say the least. Today there are many ways for fellowship members to connect, and a primary way of getting active is staying connected with other fellowship members.

Participants most likely will not like everyone or identify with everyone they meet at Twelve Step meetings. A Twelve Step adage that can be a useful guide in dealing with this reality goes like this: "Take what works and leave the rest." In this sense, the collective wisdom of the fellowship suggests gravitating toward other, more relatable members and ideas. It also suggests detaching from those whom one is uncomfortable being around. Because of the diversity inherent in Twelve Step fellowships, the more meetings (and the greater the variety of meetings) a participant attends, the more likely it is that he or she will eventually connect with at least a few people. The chances of this happening are much greater if the participant gets active at meetings.

Once participants find meetings they are comfortable attending, the next goal becomes networking. The more people participants meet and talk to, the more contacts they are likely to get—and therefore the larger the social network they will have to turn to at critical times and the times in between. Selecting a home meeting, a meeting group that is regularly attended, is a good way to start networking and building relationships that extend beyond the fellowship itself. At home meetings, networking might involve asking other members for their cell phone numbers or email addresses. It's important for participants to reach out to others when they feel lonely, angry, or depressed, but it is also important to develop friendships that can lead to socializing.

Clinical research has firmly established that a person's social network exerts a powerful effect on whether that person remains abstinent.[7] Many participants have a social network that condones or encourages substance use. If this remains their only social network, their chances of remaining abstinent are lessened substantially. Starting to build an alternative social network—one that supports recovery—is therefore vital. Twelve Step fellowships constitute that alternative social network.

Sponsorship

One of AA's oldest traditions is the use of sponsors. At first, sponsors played a rather limited role in recovery. They consisted of currently sober alcoholics who visited alcoholics in the hospital and took them to an AA meeting when they were discharged. Now all Twelve Step fellowships incorporate sponsorship into their traditions, but the role of contemporary sponsorship is very different. Today, sponsors generally do not visit inpatients or take them to meetings upon discharge. Today's sponsors largely serve as sources of advice and information for people less experienced with recovery. Sponsors educate sponsees regarding Twelve Step Traditions and the concept of "working" the Twelve Steps. They also offer advice and suggestions based on their own experience and wisdom. For example, it is common for a sponsor to ask a new sponsee to "check in" via phone, text, or email daily.

A sponsor is someone the participant can call on (in addition to other fellowship friends) who supports reliance on a fellowship of peers as the bedrock of recovery. Newcomers are encouraged to ask for a "temporary sponsor" as soon as possible, and, as mentioned earlier, they should be prepared for that sponsor to ask for frequent (often daily) contact. In time, the sponsor may also help to steer the newcomer toward helpful meetings, helpful readings, and other helpful resources. A sponsor can also encourage getting active in other ways.

One study showed the value of sponsorship to men and women in AA. Newcomers to the fellowship were tracked for one year to compare the outcomes of those who got a sponsor early (within three months) and those who waited longer (four to six months). Getting a sponsor early (recommended in the Twelve Step tradition) increased the likelihood of remaining abstinent at six months threefold.[8] In fact, research has shown that individuals with high sponsorship involvement were *seven times* more likely to remain abstinent than those with low sponsorship involvement, independent of how many meetings they attended.[9] It is good to get a sponsor early and to maintain a relationship with a sponsor.

Obtaining a sponsor can be difficult. In some areas, sponsors are inundated with requests for sponsorship. This can happen, for example, when Twelve Step meeting attendance is court mandated. At times, it is not just meeting attendance that is mandated, but sponsorship as well. Although research shows that both attending meetings and getting a sponsor are positively associated with recovery, that research was conducted with voluntary involvement. It is unknown whether the outcomes of a mandated approach are the same. Regardless, circumstances where a sponsor is asked to sponsor twenty (or even more) court-mandated individuals are not conducive to developing a meaningful sponsor-sponsee relationship.

It is simultaneously a privilege and a responsibility to be a sponsor. Sponsorship is a core aspect of the Twelfth Step, which asks those in recovery to "give back" to others what they themselves have benefited from. Sponsors should have sustained abstinence supported by their own involvement in a Twelve Step fellowship.

A sponsor understands from personal experience the agonies of addiction and the conflicts that face newly recovering individuals. He or she guides the sponsee toward getting active and beginning to work the Steps but explains how the "One day at a time" principle can help. A good sponsor sincerely cares about the sponsee, is an ally, and has expectations. But good sponsorship also involves "caring detachment," the space for the sponsee to run his or her own life without judgment.

It is important to establish healthy boundaries—a sponsor should not be a best friend, an employer, a romantic partner, or a surrogate parent. The sponsor should be of the same sexual identity as the sponsee. A sponsor is not a facilitator or a judge. A good sponsor does not dictate to a sponsee (although he or she may very well offer suggestions or state an expectation for the relationship, such as frequent contact). No formal credentials are required to become a sponsor, and it is natural to be cautious when seeking one. Just as in other spheres (e.g., psychotherapy, medical treatment), it is possible that there may be sponsors who are predators. Sponsorship requires trust, and therefore deserves a measured, carefully considered approach by both the sponsor and the sponsee.

Recovery Tasks

As always, at the end of this session, the facilitator seeks to get commitments to attend Twelve Step meetings of the participant's choice.

It may also be important to discuss any realistic obstacles to keeping this commitment (child care, transportation, and so on) and how they might be overcome. Participants are encouraged to get sponsors, and to get them sooner rather than later. Again, role-playing asking for a temporary sponsor can be very helpful when working with socially anxious participants. Continued reading of conference-approved Twelve Step fellowship literature is recommended, alongside any other readings suggested by the facilitator. Participants also identify things they will do to get active before the next TSF session, and the importance of networking continues to be stressed. The participant workbooks help with reviewing content, tracking sober days, and analyzing slips.

■ ■ ■

10

Elective Topic 1: Genograms

DIMENSION	KEY CONCEPT	CORE PROCESS	MARKERS
Social/ Behavioral	Getting active	Building a support network	• Active participation • Sponsor • Home group
Cognitive	Denial	Acceptance and surrender	• Identifying as a recovering person • Acceptance of abstinence as a personal goal
Spiritual	Personal growth	Spiritual awakening	• Moral inventory • Prayer/meditation • Altruism • Spiritual activities

The TSF elective program allows facilitators to customize the treatment plan to meet the needs of a particular participant or group. The TSF program does not approach treatment in a one-size-fits-all fashion but is instead designed to allow for individualized treatment planning. The elective topics are intended to support and strengthen personal insight along with active involvement in Twelve Step fellowships—the topics can help participants or groups to become more active with fellowships. The elective topics also address common barriers to recovery, such as emotions and social situations that can "trigger" a slip or relapse. Participant or group barriers to recovery will become apparent through the course of treatment, and the elective topics allow the program to be tailored to those needs. As mentioned previously, it may take multiple sessions to cover one topic. One or more elective topics can be incorporated into individual or group treatment plans, as appropriate and as time permits.

Genograms

Genograms combine elements of genealogical family trees with elements of social history to produce a visual intergenerational representation of family relationships pertaining to a particular subject. Genograms can be used to highlight virtually any issue or dynamic within a family. They can be used, for example, to examine family patterns in marriage and career choices, in lifestyle, in violence, or in parenting styles. In family therapy, genograms have been used extensively to help participants and therapists gain a better understanding of how traits (extroversion, creativity, ambition, and so on) as well as problems (violence, substance use, depression, and so on) are perpetuated, and to visually represent the participant's choice to break free from family patterns and build a different, healthier lifestyle. Genograms have the potential to relieve guilt and shame ("I'm not the only one in my family tree to have this problem"; "I can see how my family has perpetuated this problem").

The primary purpose of Elective Topic 1: Genograms is to examine where substance use disorders are indicated in other family members. A dramatic visual representation of patterns of alcohol and other drug use in a participant's family can help to motivate him or her to break a destructive intergenerational family cycle through actively working a Twelve Step program. How much substance use disorders can be attributed to biology versus socialization is less relevant to this discussion than the idea that participants are not alone and that they have the ability to recover from a substance use disorder.

Constructing a genogram may sound innocent enough—like building a family tree—but it has the potential to evoke intense emotional reactions, particularly if participants realize that they represent one in a long string of family members with substance use problems. Sometimes these reactions are immediate and powerful. They can lead to relief; alternatively, they can provoke a sense of hopelessness. It is not uncommon for genograms to have their greatest emotional impact after a session is over, when participants have time to reflect. Therefore, following up on this topic is important. In a group format, this topic may be spread over several sessions, depending on time constraints, with the advantage of group members seeing the patterns of substance use problems reflected in their peers' families as well as their own.

A genogram is best constructed using a whiteboard or flipchart (and is copied by the participant into his or her workbook), though a large piece of paper will do if neither is available. A participant names the members of his or her immediate family and provides information on those relationships. The genogram should include at least three generations, starting with the participant's generation and building (up and down) from there. Place each family member in the appropriate position on the genogram to create a family tree (see figure 2 on page 110). Use squares to symbolize males and circles for females. It can be helpful to include each person's current age (or age at death) within each circle or square. With deceased family members, it can also be helpful to list the cause of death, such as cancer or liver failure.

For each family member listed, the participant should provide information on the following set of questions related to substance use so that it can be filled in on the genogram. Move through each generation, including the participant's parents, uncles, and aunts. Obtain as much information as possible about the generation twice removed—the participant's grandparents. If the participant has children, obtain information about his or her children's use of alcohol and other drugs. Even if he or she does not have children or if the children are young, this is an opportunity to reflect on how family behavior can influence younger generations.

- Do the participant's family members have problems with substance use? Are they big drinkers or drug users?
- Which family member(s)?
- What substances do they use?
- What negative consequences have they experienced that might be related to their substance use?
  - legal (such as impaired driving arrests)
  - social (such as divorce)

– occupational (such as losing jobs or poor reviews)

– physical (such as health problems, overdose)

– emotional/psychological (such as depression or suicide)

– financial (such as chronic money problems or bankruptcy)

Analyzing Genograms

Genograms have the potential to bring up intergenerational issues other than the ones related to substance use. The participant may be tempted to get into a discussion of any number of meaningful collateral issues, such as family violence or legal problems. While perfectly legitimate issues, they are best addressed in a different therapeutic forum. The importance of keeping the discussion focused on substance use and its consequences cannot be emphasized enough. When other issues are raised in the discussion about the genogram, they should be correlated to substance use. Allow the discussion even if it cannot be immediately shifted back to substance use, but try to relate the discussion to substance use and its effects.

Genogram exercises also have the potential to stir up memories and emotions that may have lain dormant for years. Sudden and painful recollections of growing up in an alcoholic home, of abuse, of abandonment, or of neglect can evoke intense feelings of anger, anxiety, and shame. TSF program facilitation may not be the best environment to work through all participant concerns. Nevertheless, the program facilitator should be sensitive to the difficulties facing individual participants, and program sessions should offer helpful guidance. Emotional reactions should be validated, and participants should be guided toward Twelve Step fellowships as sources of support (some members may have had similar experiences). Participants might experience urges to drink or use as a result of this exercise, and discussion at this point should include what he or she could do about it. Participants may be referred to appropriate concurrent treatment, such as a group for survivors of sexual abuse or counseling with a therapist who is supportive of Twelve Step fellowships. Other options include speaking to a trusted fellowship member, a sponsor, a faith leader, or another friend about this exercise and the emotional reactions the participant had to it.

A balance should be struck between addressing problematic issues in the genogram and highlighting the positive aspects of family life that the genogram raises. It is reasonable to encourage the participant to honor his or her family for strengths despite acknowledging the harm done through substance use. This will allow flashes of brightness now and then during what might otherwise be a grim topic that raises feelings of shame and despair. Negative reactions should be validated, such as anxiety, depression, and hopelessness, but replicating family patterns or breaking them is a choice (and opportunity) that should be stressed.

Malik: Analyzing a Genogram

Malik was suspended as a result of being drunk on the job. He also had an arrest for driving while intoxicated. As a result of his suspension, he was referred for a substance use evaluation. Now forty-five, he'd been drinking more or less since he was a teenager. The progression of his alcohol use disorder had been gradual and insidious. His job brought him into frequent contact with heavy drinkers, many of whom drank at lunch and occasionally on the job. His tolerance was formidable—even his wife reported that she rarely saw him visibly drunk. Still, when he was arrested, his blood alcohol level was three times above the legal limit. He said this had been a typical evening for him in terms of how much he drank.

When he first came for the evaluation, Malik readily admitted that he had a drinking problem. At the same time, he minimized its severity in comparison to that of other men he knew. He flatly rejected the idea that he had an alcohol use disorder, despite the fact that he frequently drove under the influence, had a problem with high blood pressure, and "didn't feel normal" until he had that first drink after work.

Although Malik's substance use was limited to alcohol, he was aware that others in his family used other substances—most notably cannabis, but also prescription medications for pain and anxiety. An asterisk beside a person's name in Malik's genogram denotes that he or she had a known substance use problem. A question mark denotes someone in whom a substance use problem was suspected based on the information Malik provided.

Figure 2. Sample Genogram for Malik

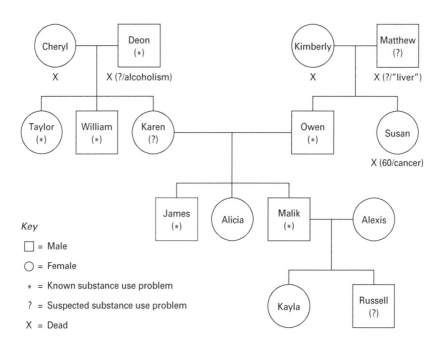

Key

☐ = Male

○ = Female

∗ = Known substance use problem

? = Suspected substance use problem

X = Dead

Malik's genogram outlines three generations of alcoholism. Malik's maternal grandfather, Deon; his maternal uncle, William, and maternal aunt, Taylor; his father, Owen; and his younger brother, James, all had acknowledged drinking problems. In addition, Malik reported that James had also been a regular user of marijuana for years. William had a history of losing jobs, had been through alcohol detoxification more than once, and had a heart condition that was most likely linked to his drinking. Taylor had been married and divorced, was still a drinker, and lived with her son and his wife. Taylor was known to use a lot of anxiety medication "for her nerves." His maternal grandfather, Deon, had been a notorious drunk whose temper Malik's mother, Karen, and her siblings had feared. His mother had told him once that all three siblings would hide beneath their beds whenever their father came staggering in after a bender. He was universally hated and was widely known to have drunk himself to death.

On his father's side, Malik identified his own father, Owen, as a man who drank more as he aged, although Malik justified this as a reaction to the stress from having to care for his wife, Karen, who had been chronically ill, in addition to having to work "endless" hours in their family business in order to support them. Malik could not remember ever seeing his father seemingly drunk, nor had the man ever been abusive. "I think he was one of those quiet drunks—like me," Malik said.

On reflection, Malik said that his mother had many doctors, and he suspected that she may have misused medications. The thought had never occurred to him, though, that misuse of prescription drugs might have contributed to her chronically poor health. Malik knew little about his paternal grandfather, Matthew, although he did know that Matthew had died at a relatively early age "of some kind of liver problem." And he had once overheard his mother tell someone else that her father-in-law "liked his liquor."

Finally, Malik and his wife, Alexis, had two children, Russell and Kayla. Six months before Malik's arrest, Russell had also been arrested for driving while intoxicated and had his license suspended. Though Malik and Alexis had spoken little about it, Malik suspected she was angry at him over Russell's incident. He acknowledged that his own drinking hadn't presented a good role model for his son to follow, and he felt worried about Russell.

Malik was noticeably subdued after completing his genogram. During his next TSF session, he started out by saying that he had "reconsidered things." "I guess you could say that booze runs through my family," he said. "And it has been making my life somewhat unmanageable, as AA says. I think maybe I should think about giving it up."

Recovery Tasks

At the end of this session, the participant is asked to spend some time reflecting on the results of his or her genogram, and to consider sharing thoughts during the next session. The participant also commits to attend Twelve Step meetings of his or her choice. If the participant does not yet have a sponsor, he or she should be encouraged to take steps before the next session to get one. Additional coaching and role-playing exercises around asking for a sponsor may be appropriate. Participants are encouraged to continue their networking efforts. Continued reading of conference-approved Twelve Step fellowship literature is recommended, alongside any other readings suggested by the facilitator. The participant workbooks help with reviewing content, tracking sober days, and analyzing slips.

■ ■ ■

11

Elective Topic 2: Enabling

DIMENSION	KEY CONCEPT	CORE PROCESS	MARKERS
Social/ Behavioral	Getting active	Building a support network	• Active participation • Sponsor • Home group
Cognitive	Denial	Acceptance and surrender	• Identifying as a recovering person • Acceptance of abstinence as a personal goal
Spiritual	Personal growth	Spiritual awakening	• Moral inventory • Prayer/meditation • Altruism • Spiritual activities

Enabling can be defined as any and all behaviors by others that have the effect of facilitating continued drinking or using, or that have helped someone struggling with addiction to avoid or minimize the negative consequences related to substance use. In other words, enablers provide the means, the excuses, and the safety net that allow someone with a substance use disorder to continue using. The material in Elective Topic 2: Enabling examines how well a participant understands the concept of enabling, explains the dynamics of enabling, and explores an enabling inventory. While an enabling inventory looks at specific enabling patterns in a participant's life, the concept of performing a self-inventory is useful for Steps Four and Ten of the Twelve Steps. Additionally, material from this topic can be helpful for Steps Eight and Nine. This topic is helpful during the process of acceptance and surrender, but it also relates to personal growth and the recovery markers associated with it.

It is helpful to start this topic with a discussion on what enabling means to the participant or group. This discussion ensures that participants have a clear understanding of the concept; the illustration of a few examples can be useful. Some examples include friends or partners who

- offer alcohol and other drugs when someone's already under the influence
- ensure they have enough alcohol and other drugs around to share
- make light of getting drunk or high often
- obtain substances for others to use
- lend money for alcohol and other drugs
- make excuses for others when they're intoxicated
- nurse others when they're hungover

Enabling

Enabling can take many forms. For example, when the consequences of substance use are managed by someone else, such as a parent, spouse, or loved one, the full impact might not be seen and felt by the one struggling with a substance use disorder. This can lead to continued use and more negative consequences.

> The convulsions she had had at home were so thoroughly covered up by me that she could not remember them the next day. I massaged her, poured honey down her throat, soothed her and applied cold compresses. It proved futile to tell her what had occurred because, within a short time, the drinking began again. It is now clear to me that it is necessary for the alcoholic to feel the pain. But it was I who bore my daughter's pain. I deprived her of some of the incentive to take constructive action for the consequences of her drinking. In essence, I took on the responsibility and the consequences of her disease.
>
> —*Al-Anon Faces Alcoholism* [1]

Another example may involve indulgence or pampering. It can be motivated by caring and concern, or it may reflect the enabler's own desire to deny reality.

> False pride helped me create a prison in which I lived for the next twenty years. I wanted to be proud of our marriage and our family (we had six sons), so I buried the resentment and began pretending. By the time our sons were in their twenties, one had gone through treatment for chemical dependency. I also realized that three of our other sons were also substance abusers. I didn't want to believe this was happening or that alcohol or drugs was the problem. So I kept on pretending and I played the role of caretaker for the whole family. I assumed it was my job to control them, make them happy, to keep them from hurting and out of trouble. The family seemed to agree. Their dependent personalities accepted such mothering and only occasionally did they rebel.
>
> *—Anonymous*[2]

In some instances, enabling appears intentional; for example, when a spouse says, "She is chilled out when she drinks and takes her anxiety medication, even though it's too much of both. But at least she is easier to live with." Or "He's less irritable after he's had a few drinks." In most instances, however, enabling mirrors addiction—it is something that a person slips into gradually and insidiously over time. Generally speaking, enablers *do not intend* to facilitate or promote a substance use problem any more than the substance user sets out to do so. In fact, the individual with a substance use disorder needs to take some responsibility for creating his or her enabling network.

Addiction and enabling can evolve into psychologically complementary processes. As a dependent person, the individual with a substance use disorder needs the enabler, who in turn "needs to be needed." Most of the time, neither the person with a substance use disorder nor the enabler set out with the goal of establishing this unhealthy dynamic. However defined, enabling serves to mitigate the negative consequences of addiction and thereby has the (often unintended) effect of hindering someone with a substance use disorder from taking necessary actions toward successful treatment and recovery.

The Enabler

Enabling behavior is fairly easy to discern, but the underlying motivations for enabling may be complex and less apparent. Most people become enablers not because they *want* the person with a substance use disorder to continue drinking or using, but because they desire to *protect* him or her out of a sense of responsibility and duty. A person's motives for enabling are usually benign and loving, but the enabler's behavior ends up being mutually destructive to the person with the addiction and the person who is enabling. Nonetheless, the good intentions are important to keep in mind since the term *enabler* may have pejorative associations for some people.

Enablers sometimes feel guilty because they believe that they have somehow caused or contributed to the substance use problem. This is particularly true for parents, who may torture themselves with self-recriminations about what they did wrong or what they should have done differently. Enabling partners can be vulnerable to self-doubts regarding their adequacy within the relationship. Enablers may be fearful and anxious because they worry about what might happen if they stop enabling—perhaps, ironically, because they are afraid that the person with the substance use disorder will abandon them if they do. The person with a substance use disorder, caught in a web of addiction, may in fact play off this guilt in order to promote continued substance use and continued enabling.

Sooner or later, enablers come to feel depressed and hopeless from the futility of their enabling and the progression of the substance use disorder. At that point, the enabler may resort to alienation, which can gradually undermine the viability of the relationship. Enablers themselves may turn to substance use, to food, or to work as a compensation for the pain they feel. For these reasons, enablers need healing and recovery as much as those with substance use disorders do. Counseling may be a good place to begin an enabler's own recovery, as well as "fellowships for the affected," such as Al-Anon, Nar-Anon, and Alateen.

Enabling Inventory

This activity is an important part of both the cognitive and the behavioral recovery processes, and also the personal growth associated with recovery. Constructing an enabling inventory involves having the participant list enabling people close to him or her. Learning how to perform a self-inventory is a skill in and of itself, and this may be the first time that participants have ever undertaken an activity of this sort—it can be uncomfortable for many. Participants may be reluctant to admit just how much their problems with substance use have been actively facilitated by friends or loved ones in addition to the role they themselves have played in promoting enabling. Because of this, this activity may need to be continued over two or more sessions.

Specific examples of enabling behavior are examined in order to understand how participants have felt enabled, and afterward participants identify the ways in which they have actively encouraged the enabling behaviors. By actively performing a self-inventory, participants learn a skill that can be handy in Steps Four, Five, and Ten of the Twelve Steps. The inventory activity in Elective Topic 2: Enabling may provide foundational knowledge and encouragement for participants to use as they "work" the Twelve Steps with the guidance and support of fellowships.

Recovery Tasks

At the end of this session, participants are encouraged to reflect on their enabling inventory, and further thoughts can be shared during future sessions. Participants are asked to commit to attending Twelve Step meetings of their choice. If a participant does not yet have a sponsor, he or she should be encouraged to take steps before the next session to get one. If necessary, role-play asking for a temporary sponsor. Participants are encouraged to continue their networking efforts. Continued reading of conference-approved Twelve Step fellowship literature is recommended, alongside any other readings suggested by the facilitator. The participant workbooks help with reviewing content, tracking sober days, and analyzing slips.

■ ■ ■

12

Elective Topic 3: People, Places, and Routines

DIMENSION	KEY CONCEPT	CORE PROCESS	MARKERS
Social/ Behavioral	Getting active	Building a support network	• Active participation • Sponsor • Home group
Cognitive	Denial	Acceptance and surrender	• Identifying as a recovering person • Acceptance of abstinence as a personal goal
Spiritual	Personal growth	Spiritual awakening	• Moral inventory • Prayer/meditation • Altruism • Spiritual activities

Whereas Core Topic 4: Getting Active in Twelve Step Fellowships provides an introduction to the social/behavioral recovery dimension, Elective Topic 3: People, Places, and Routines takes a more in-depth approach and bridges the material with the cognitive recovery dimension. This topic is intended to address some of the practicalities of staying abstinent—what participants can do about spending time with friends who drink or use, about going to parties, about changing habits intimately associated with substance use, and so on. It is unrealistic for anyone with a substance use disorder to expect the world to change in response to his or her intention to stay sober; rather, those with a substance use disorder must change their lifestyle in order to stay sober. Recovery requires fundamental changes in attitudes and behaviors.

Facilitation of TSF and TSF-COD should be pragmatic, flexible, and nondogmatic. The goal is to discover ways for participants to stay sober in difficult situations. A common saying within Twelve Step fellowships is "To avoid slipping, avoid slippery people, slippery places, and slippery things." It is helpful to start Elective Topic 3: People, Places, and Routines by reading this quote and asking participants how they relate to it personally, since a decision to make lifestyle changes is contingent on this basic insight.

Recovery Lifestyles

The quote mentioned earlier captures one of the most useful pieces of advice that Twelve Step fellowships have to offer those seeking recovery: As a substance use disorder progresses in severity, lifestyle changes progress as well. Habits, social networks, and many other aspects of daily living come to accommodate substance use over time. These changes can be simple, such as making sure there is cold wine or beer in the fridge—or a supply of marijuana or pain medication—for when the individual gets home from work. Or they can be more complex, such as the progressive drift away from old friends in favor of new ones who drink or use.

Twelve Step fellowships are rooted in a tradition of pragmatism—*what works.* Bill Wilson devoted much time over many years to answering practical questions from recovering alcoholics about how to stay sober in various situations. His strategy, which has become an integral part of Twelve Step culture, was to share "suggestions" that others had found helpful in those same situations, but to make it clear that the decision to follow or not follow those suggestions was strictly up to the individual.[1]

> Certain set times, familiar places, and regular activities associated with drinking have been woven closely into the fabric of our lives. Like fatigue, hunger, loneliness, anger, and overelation, these old routines can prove to be traps dangerous to our sobriety.
>
> —*Living Sober*[2]

Participants with substance use disorders have gravitated toward a social network of men and women who use or support use. In fact, participants have likely developed a range of habits and rituals associated with substance use. Some of these rituals may involve daily routines, such as cooking, cleaning, coming home from work, or watching television while drinking or getting high. Other rituals may involve certain people, places, or even items of clothing.

The process of connecting use with particular people, places, things, and routines happens naturally as use becomes habitual. Those with substance use disorders are increasingly preoccupied with maintaining an amount of the substance in their bodies, but they are also intimately connected with rituals. Engaging in the rituals themselves leads to feelings of eager anticipation; disrupting these rituals leads to anxiety and anger.

In a sense, we are all creatures of habit. Changing habits, no matter how mundane, is no easy matter. In order to stay abstinent, participants need to change a lot of patterns associated with habitual use. Otherwise, their willpower will be no match for the combined power of routine ritual and the obsession with the substance.

Sam: Keeping a Daily Ritual

Sam had been smoking marijuana daily for seventeen years and had developed a complex ritual surrounding his use. A midlevel manager by day, he would never smoke until after work. But as soon as he left the office and got to his car, the first thing he would do was remove his tie. Then he'd start music in the car—music that he liked to listen to when he was high, but that he never played until he was ready to get high. By the time he was out of the company parking lot, his first joint would be lit. By the time he got home, which took about forty minutes, he'd be finished with the joint.

Sam changed his clothes before lighting a second joint. Sam liked wearing the same clothes when he was high—old jeans and flannel shirts. He'd retreat into a small den he'd created—his "man cave"—light the second joint, and carefully roll another for the next day. Sam was married with two teenage children; his wife had long ago given up complaining about the marijuana use. On those occasions when she had,

Sam had responded defensively and angrily. He argued that he never missed a day of work (which was true) and used this as evidence that his pot use was "harmless." He didn't recognize that his daily pot use had rendered him all but inaccessible to his wife and children.

If anything happened to disrupt Sam's marijuana routine, he immediately became irritated. For example, he didn't want to be bothered about household issues when he got home from work. He said those could wait until later in the evening. The same held for any issues his kids were having—at school or with their peers. These too could wait until after he'd had time to "unwind." Over time, Sam's wife took responsibility for all the household issues, and his children never talked to him.

One night, Sam and his wife were awakened by a call from their older son, Jason. He'd taken his father's Jeep and swerved to avoid a deer while driving down a local dirt road that was a shortcut to home. He hit a large dirt bump and tipped the Jeep over. He was okay, he said, but needed help. When Sam and his wife arrived at the scene, the police were there. They'd already called a tow truck to right the Jeep so that it could be towed to a garage. Sam, of course, was stoned. When the police spoke with him, his wife could see that they knew this, since they asked who was going to drive Jason home. Humiliated, she said she would. And when Jason got into the car, it was obvious that he too knew that his father was stoned. No one spoke on the drive home.

The next night, Sam found his wife and Jason waiting for him when he got home from work. Before he could retreat to his den, they confronted him. What they said was simple: Had Sam gone to the scene of the accident alone, he would have been arrested. That meant that the family could not count on Sam in a time of crisis. He needed to seriously think about his pot use and how it was affecting the family, including the loss of respect that it created.

Rituals and Routines Inventory

The rituals and routines inventory (also known as the "People, Places, and Routines Inventory") is important to both the social and cognitive recovery domains. Constructing a rituals and routines inventory involves writing down the people, places, and routines that have come to be associated with (and support) substance use and that must therefore be changed in order to build a robust recovery. Participants may just be learning how to perform an activity like this, and it does not always come easy. Like other TSF topics, this one may be spread out over multiple sessions.

Performing a rituals and routines inventory uses skills that are also helpful in Steps Four, Five, Eight, Nine, and Ten of the Twelve Steps. In that sense, this activity may become the base knowledge necessary for participants as they "work" the Twelve Steps with the guidance and support of fellowships.

The goal is to identify social networks, rituals, and routines and record them on a whiteboard, with participants copying this information into their workbooks. It's helpful to discuss specific information, and the more you write down, the better. Detailed sequences of events that participants follow before they use are important. Members of their social network who enable substance use are important (for example, more than one person in early recovery has made the decision to change their cell phone number and clear all contacts in order to make it more difficult to contact old friends who use). Routines should be examined thoroughly, again probing for details. Identifying these details helps participants determine how much of their lives revolves around substance use: whom they spend time with, what habits they have, how powerful rituals and routines can be, and how habitual behaviors can defeat their own willpower.

One woman identified ironing as an everyday activity that she did while drinking half a bottle of wine. A salesman drank every night as he went over his orders and receipts for the day. And yet another woman would retreat to her bedroom, where she kept her stockpile of pain medications carefully hidden, and after taking one she'd sit in a comfortable chair and read a novel.

After completing a rituals and routines inventory, the next step is to find substitutes for the people, places, rituals, and routines that support substance use. This is done through an activity in which participants create a Recovery Lifestyle Contract.

Recovery Lifestyle Contract

Generally speaking, it is easier for people to give up or change an old habit if they are able to replace it with a new one. Finding substitutes for the people, places, rituals, and routines that support substance use is not easy. Giving something up—especially something important—leaves a gaping hole in a person's lifestyle. Creating a Recovery Lifestyle Contract can help the participant overcome this problem. Again, a whiteboard is useful, and participants should copy the information into their workbooks.

The purpose of the Recovery Lifestyle Contract is to help participants develop a blueprint for change—a list of what needs to be given up and what could be substituted for it. Without both parts of the contract in place, the participant is apt to fail. In other words, giving up old habits associated with use will not work in the long run unless they are replaced with new, recovery-associated habits. Therefore, after identifying the people, places, things, routines, and rituals in their lives that support substance use, participants create a list of sober people to spend more time with, places and activities to participate in that are substance free (including Twelve Step fellowship meetings and activities), things in their environment that trigger urges and need to be removed and replaced, and new, substance-free routines and rituals that need to be established.

When creating a Recovery Lifestyle Contract, it is important to concentrate on small, specific change commitments that the participant can make and follow up on in later sessions. Asking participants to immediately leave all of their enabling relationships, for example, may be too large a leap to make. Instead, brainstorming with and coaching participants about changes they might make and how those changes could help support recovery is likely to be more productive.

Change and Grief

Elective Topic 3: People, Places, and Routines can involve a great deal of resistance from participants. Like Core Topic 4: Getting Active in Twelve Step Fellowships, this topic pushes participants to commit themselves to making behavioral changes. Those changes involve giving up friendships, habits, and well-established rituals in order to develop new ones.

Even though participants may identify the need to make these changes, in practice it is easier said than done. In other words, talk is cheap, but action can be costly.

These changes may sound straightforward on the surface, but the emotional impact of the Recovery Lifestyle Contract should not be minimized. A lifestyle is hard to let go of—small wonder that this topic is challenging for participants. To help overcome this resistance, it can be helpful to recognize the grief associated with losses during this change process.

It is natural for people to grieve over the loss of old friends, old habits, old hangouts, and old activities. The participant who minimizes the impact of these losses may be in a state of denial, or he or she may be participating in the topic to placate the facilitator without any real intention of following through.

A common exercise in substance use disorder treatment programs is to have participants write good-bye letters to substances, expressing grief over having to give up this relationship. Such letters can be written to many of the things that the participant must give up in the interest of recovery. The participant can write a good-bye letter to his or her best enabling friends, to music that he or she associates with substance use, or to places where he or she used to use.

It can also be helpful to emphasize gains alongside the losses. Think of the saying "When a son marries, his parents gain a daughter." The wisdom in this saying is also appropriate for the man or woman in recovery. The individual who fully embraces Twelve Step culture learns that there are easily as many gains as losses in the long run, such as conscious, clear-headed living; new, trustworthy friends; spiritual renewal; self-esteem—these are only a few of the gains that can be realized through recovery. Achieving the gains requires that participants give up some things, but it can be helpful to remember the negative consequences that came with those things they are losing.

Feelings of grief evoked by this session are legitimate and should be recognized. Yet some balance needs to be provided to participant outlooks. Hope can be instilled through the specific, practical benefits that recovery has to offer, rather than general or abstract assurances. New relationships will emerge to replace old ones, and new interests will develop to replace old ones too. This perspective can help participants experience grief without despair, and the anxiety of loss may be offset by the excitement of new opportunities.

Adolescent Considerations

One's peer group plays a crucial role during adolescent development, so adolescents with substance use disorders have important considerations on this topic. It is during adolescence that our identity crystallizes—our sense of who we are, where we belong, what we stand for, and what our options are for the future. Teens typically experiment with (or at least fantasize about) belonging to different peer groups. Some of these function well and will be good influences on healthy adulthood. These are peer groups composed of generally successful teens who have positive self-esteem, have a realistic sense of their own talents and interests, and set personal goals based on these talents and interests. Unfortunately, teens can also gravitate toward less functional peer groups, such as those with high substance use rates. Teens with substance use disorders often already have a peer group that engages in substance use. This group likely provides a sense of belonging—even though it very likely also shares a bleak or unrealistic outlook for the future. Teens in treatment often report that the sole activity that bonds these peer groups is getting high together. Treatment efforts need to address these issues, because teens leaving treatment are at risk of gravitating back to the peer group they used substances with. This accounts for exceptionally high relapse rates reported for adolescents with substance use disorders.

Twelve Step fellowships offer an alternative peer support group for teens in recovery. However, it can be a therapeutic challenge to steer teens toward a more functional (and hopeful) identity and peer group. Therefore, it is highly recommended that Elective Topic 3: People, Places, and Routines be a central part of a treatment plan for adolescents with substance use disorders. For this reason, getting active in Twelve Step fellowships becomes an important recovery task as well.

Recovery Tasks

At the end of this session, participants are asked to consider changes from their Recovery Lifestyle Contract that they can make. Reflection on the Recovery Lifestyle Contract is important, and follow-ups can be shared during future sessions. Participants are asked to commit to attending Twelve Step meetings of their choice. If a participant does not yet have a sponsor, he or she should be encouraged to take steps before the next session to get one. Participants are encouraged to continue their networking efforts. Continued reading of conference-approved Twelve Step fellowship literature is recommended, alongside any other readings suggested by the facilitator. The participant workbooks help with reviewing content, tracking sober days, and analyzing slips.

■ ■ ■

Elective Topic 4: Emotions

DIMENSION	KEY CONCEPT	CORE PROCESS	MARKERS
Social/ Behavioral	Getting active	Building a support network	• Active participation • Sponsor • Home group
Cognitive	Denial	Acceptance and surrender	• Identifying as a recovering person • Acceptance of abstinence as a personal goal
Spiritual	Personal growth	Spiritual awakening	• Moral inventory • Prayer/meditation • Altruism • Spiritual activities

Elective Topic 4: Emotions helps identify difficult emotions that trigger urges for substance use. Learning to identify emotions is a step toward personal growth, but it is also a step toward managing difficult emotions without substance use. The ability to manage difficult emotions while abstinent is part of identifying as a recovering person—an indicator of progress in the cognitive recovery dimension. Trigger emotions are often set off by conscious or unconscious thought processes, which reiterate this topic's emphasis on the cognitive recovery domain. For example, on a conscious level, a strong dislike for someone can lead to resentment or anger; on an unconscious level, believing that one's situation is hopeless, or that life is meaningless, can trigger depression, loneliness, or ennui.

Many seek out substance use to help them manage difficult emotions. Over time, this can lead to reliance on substance use for coping with those emotions. Alternatively, people may come to rely on substances in order to experience positive emotions. In either case, substance use and emotions become entwined. As a result, emotions can pose a high risk for slips and relapse in people with substance use disorders. Not only do newly abstinent individuals need to understand the connection between emotions and substance use but also they need to *expect that emotions they previously avoided through substance use, or pursued through substance use, will most certainly make themselves known in recovery.*

This topic begins with a discussion on how emotions relate to substance use. This helps identify which emotions are most relevant to individual participants. Participant history with substance use informs this discussion, as substance use may have been part of a coping mechanism for difficult emotions related to traumatic experiences such as abuse, neglect, or loss. Or it may be a way to relieve boredom or ennui and feel good. This discussion should reflect on how substance use affected those emotions—including how it helped participants to cope with the emotions, or how it helped participants to create them. Sometimes substance use is used as a crutch that prevents the development of healthy responses to emotions, such as the ability to feel comfortable and have fun in social environments without relying on alcohol and other drugs. Many emotions can come up through facilitation of this topic, so it may be necessary to spread facilitation out over multiple sessions.

Twelve Step fellowships have long recognized the connection between emotions and substance use. Because of this, Twelve Step fellowships are a great resource for support in managing difficult emotions. Indeed, much of Twelve Step conference-approved literature deals with handling difficult emotions. Many Twelve Step slogans relate to coping with difficult emotions by offering advice on alternative ways of thinking ("Easy does it," "Let go and let God," "One day at a time," "First things first," "Turn it over"), as does the Serenity Prayer. These slogans and sayings do not necessarily solve problems, but their value lies in their simplicity and truth. They offer practical bits of wisdom on how to deal with difficult emotions in alternative ways. They can help an individual see a situation from a different perspective. These slogans have helped countless Twelve Step fellowship members to cope without resorting to substance use. They are also consistent with cognitive-behavioral therapy, as described earlier.

Rick: Burying Emotions

Rick was just seventeen and had many symptoms of severe alcohol and other drug problems when he was admitted to a Twelve Step–oriented treatment program. That happened because he was confronted by his parents after totaling the family car he'd been allowed to use. He skidded off the road into a tree. Though he tried to blame it on road conditions, his parents—to their credit—would have none of it. They were aware of his drinking, though he vehemently denied drinking while driving. They told Rick how lucky he was that, after a frantic phone call, it was they who found him instead of the police. He was home before they reported the incident. But his parents insisted that he go in for an evaluation of his alcohol use or else forego driving for a year.

At his intake interview, Rick tried to minimize his substance use at first. This interview was conducted by a substance use treatment professional, but two teen peer counselors also attended—one male and one female. They were alumni of the treatment program. Confronted by them, eventually Rick admitted to drinking at least a six-pack of beer every day for the past two years. To pay for his drinking, he used money he earned from a part-time job as well as money he stole from his parents. He also admitted to smoking marijuana daily for nearly as long, and he admitted to recently experimenting with medication for attention-deficit/hyperactivity disorder. A senior in high school who was once a solid B student, Rick's recent grades barely made him eligible for graduation. He had no plans for the future.

Rick's problems with substance use started two years earlier, a few days after his girlfriend was killed in a car accident. She'd gone out drinking with some friends, and the driver of the car had slid off the road and slammed into a tree—just as Rick had, but at a much higher speed. Two girls in the backseat survived, but the driver and Rick's girlfriend, who wasn't wearing her seat belt in the passenger seat, did not.

For the first week in treatment, Rick did fine, but then he began to have problems. His temper was short, and he got into arguments with staff and other patients. He pushed someone after that. After being confronted about his need to find a socially acceptable way of dealing with his anger, he flung a chair across the room. After another confrontation by a counselor and a group of peers, the story of Rick's girlfriend came out. It was a very emotional experience for him, and one that touched everyone in the group.

Miya: Facing the Past

At age thirty, Miya had been sober and attending both AA and NA regularly for six months when she sought personal therapy for depression. She had managed to stay abstinent, but it had come at a cost. She had lost more than twenty pounds over those six months, she had chronic sleeping problems that included nightmares, and she had anxiety attacks at work that had no apparent cause. She told her therapist that she also experienced feelings of guilt that she could not connect to anything. The guilty feelings were intense enough to make her think that she was a bad person. She even thought once about killing herself. She was resisting the urges to drink and use by attending meetings at least daily and often twice a day.

Miya's emotional distress turned out to be the result of a history of sexual abuse that spanned six years of her childhood, from ages seven to thirteen. To complicate the trauma and shame associated with the abuse itself, Miya's mother had refused to accept the truth despite blatant evidence. At one point, her mother had discovered ten-year-old Miya in bed, naked, with her husband. Her mother reacted by walking out of the room. When Miya brought it up and asked her mother for help later on, her mother lashed out by saying, "Don't you ever do that with your father again!" Miya blamed herself for somehow being seductive.

Difficult Emotions

Upon entering recovery, someone who has a substance use disorder is vulnerable to experiencing any and all emotions that they have previously sought to cope with through substance use. Facilitators should expect this and be prepared to problem-solve with participants around alternative ways to deal with those emotions. Some of the more difficult feelings encountered in recovery include loneliness, anxiety, shame, anger, boredom, guilt, grief, frustration, and resentment.

HALT

Twelve Step conference-approved literature represents the collective wisdom of fellowship groups everywhere and speaks to the experiences of many recovering individuals through the years. The AA publication *Living Sober* discusses how feeling hungry, angry, lonely, or tired (HALT) is frequently cited as a trigger for someone with a substance use disorder. In fact, substance use may be an attempt by some to mitigate difficult emotional states (angry, lonely) and difficult physical states (hungry, tired). Regarding these four feelings, *Living Sober* recommends getting enough sleep, eating frequent snacks, and discussing difficult emotions with fellow AA members or a sponsor. This helps with avoiding slips and can provide a model for how to manage other difficult emotional and physical states.

Boredom and Ennui

The emotion of boredom has particular relevance for the elderly, the infirm, and the socially isolated. It is often the result of circumstances beyond their control, such as widowhood, prolonged unemployment, or isolation from friends and family. Many elderly people fall into this last group. According to the National Council on Alcoholism and Drug Dependence (NCADD), "Alcohol and drug problems, particularly prescription drug abuse, among older adults is one of the fastest growing health problems facing the country."[1] The number of single and widowed elderly men and women separated from extended family is also increasing. Loneliness and boredom come alongside that isolation, and substance use can be a means of coping. Therefore, seniors with substance use disorders may benefit from adding some meaningful structure in their lives: going to senior centers, doing volunteer work, and so on. Attending Twelve Step fellowship meetings provides support for recovery, and it can also help the loneliness and boredom that contribute to the problem.

When teens are asked to identify the emotion that first motivated them to use substances, the overwhelming majority will say boredom. Teens with substance use disorders often have too much unstructured (and unsupervised) time on their hands. Moreover, when asked what they would like to do instead of substance use, many teens will simply shrug. This can present a significant challenge to TSF facilitation, since there is very limited access to teens' families.

Whereas teens may say that boredom motivates them to use alcohol and other drugs, there may be something deeper at play. The term *ennui* may be more descriptive for many teen substance users. *Ennui* is defined as the absence of interest, spirit, or enthusiasm. As opposed to merely being bored because of circumstances beyond their control, teens experiencing ennui are adrift, with no goals, no clearly defined values, and no connections beyond others who can be described the same way. In some ways, the solution for these teens includes a spiritual component, delving into issues like identity, values, and purpose.

In situations like this, treatment should include creating greater structure in the lives of teens with substance use disorders. This may include creative activities like art therapy, physical activities like hiking to promote regular exercise, and domestic activities like preparing meals. Bored teens may respond quickly and positively to a more structured lifestyle. While it can present logistical challenges, teens may benefit from structured after-school activities such as attending exercise or sports programs, going to athletic centers, going to community centers, volunteering, and so on. Some of these activities may include a spiritual component, such as reading and then sharing reactions to books that have particular relevance for teens, communing with art, and promoting a love of nature.

Anxiety

Untreated social anxiety disorders can be major barriers to recovery, as they stand in the way of getting involved in a fellowship. The same is true for free-floating anxiety, such as is common in post-traumatic stress disorder. Although anxiety treatment is a separate discussion, it is an important consideration as a potential barrier to recovery. Referral for concurrent treatment may be the most appropriate option.

Twelve Step fellowships are another support option, and both TSF and TSF-COD facilitation include suggestions on how to help socially anxious people get more involved (including exploring online meetings to start, attending open meetings and just listening, and role-playing with the facilitator).

Grief

Grief is another powerful emotion that often relates to addiction. The personal histories of many people with substance use disorders are marked by losses that went ungrieved. Those who specialize in treating grief say that true acceptance of loss comes slowly and usually only as denial breaks down and the individual can come to terms, without panic, with the reality of the loss. Moreover, it is only when some level of acceptance is reached that the individual is truly emotionally free. Patients in treatment for substance use disorders may find that their use provided an ineffective means of coping with loss. Stories told in Twelve Step "speaker meetings" are typically a chronicle of successive losses: of health, of personal potential, of relationships, of careers, and so on. Twelve Step fellowships provide an important support network for recovering individuals coming to terms with grief.

Anger and Resentment

Anger seems to be a pivotal emotion for some with substance use disorders. Some people with substance use disorders, for example, can relate to the idea of drinking either to find the "courage" to express anger they would ordinarily suppress, or the opposite—to prevent venting anger they are afraid to express. Ironically, alcohol tends to reduce inhibitions around both emotions and behaviors, including anger and sex, so it can and often does backfire. Cannabis, in contrast, tends to mute emotions, including anger and fear, which is one reason why so many war veterans turn to it. Once participants identify a connection between anger and substance use, assistance with problem solving can help them safely express their anger in other, healthier ways.

Twelve Step fellowships have long recognized that resentment is a trigger for substance use. Resentment seems to grow from frustration involving an unexpressed or unresolved sense of injustice. Many people "store up" resentment, and then use alcohol or other drugs to suppress it. Managing resentment can be an ongoing challenge in recovery, but some aspects worth exploring include issues or experiences that cause resentment, whether the resentment stems from injustice or disrespect; how resentment was handled; and whether it is better to address resentments or let go of them.

Finding a sympathetic ear can go a long way toward relieving resentment. For resentment based in current, ongoing relationships, problem solving can help determine the best way to address resentment in a productive way. After all, the alternative—continuing to suppress resentment—will remain a threat to recovery.

Guilt and Shame

Guilt and shame appear to be opposite sides of the same coin: We feel guilty for what we have done (or not done); we feel shame about who we are. The former has to do with actions; the latter with character. For example, a parent with a severe alcohol use disorder may carry both guilt and shame for not living up to his or her own expectations for parenthood, or for not being a good provider. Victims of sexual abuse often blame themselves, leading to both guilt ("I should have resisted") and shame ("I'm a bad person"). Alcohol and other drugs can provide temporary relief from such emotions, though they often also lead to addiction.

Suppressed guilt and shame will almost always emerge in recovery. If not addressed, these emotions can easily lead to relapse. Concurrent psychotherapy is recommended for individuals struggling with guilt and shame. In addition, once sobriety has been established and an individual is connected to a fellowship, working with someone on Steps Four, Five, Six, and Seven can help to free him or her from this emotional burden.

Recovery Tasks

At the end of this session, participants are asked to think about emotions that could trigger an urge to use and consider a way to cope with emotions in a healthier way. Participants are asked to commit to attend Twelve Step meetings of their choice. If a participant does not yet have a sponsor, he or she should be encouraged to take steps before the next session to get one. Participants are encouraged to continue their networking efforts. Continued reading of conference-approved Twelve Step fellowship literature is recommended, alongside any other readings suggested by the facilitator. The participant workbooks help with reviewing content, tracking sober days, and analyzing slips.

■ ■ ■

Elective Topic 5: Spirituality

DIMENSION	KEY CONCEPT	CORE PROCESS	MARKERS
Social/ Behavioral	Getting active	Building a support network	• Active participation • Sponsor • Home group
Cognitive	Denial	Acceptance and surrender	• Identifying as a recovering person • Acceptance of abstinence as a personal goal
Spiritual	Personal growth	Spiritual awakening	• Moral inventory • Prayer/meditation • Altruism • Spiritual activities

Elective Topic 5: Spirituality approaches the spiritual dimension of recovery in a nondenominational, pragmatic way. It starts by simply discussing the concept of spirituality and what we know about spirituality and recovery. The recovery markers of the spiritual domain are also discussed, as well as how negative religious experiences may affect someone in recovery. Additionally, both agnosticism and atheism are addressed in order to highlight how versatile spiritual interpretations can be within the TSF and TSF-COD programs. The subject matter covered in this topic is helpful in understanding a Twelve Step approach to recovery, and the knowledge can be applied by individuals working on Steps Five, Six, Seven, and Eleven.

This topic begins with a discussion on how spirituality is different from religiosity and what both mean to participants. Some helpful discussion points include distinguishing between religion and spirituality, describing spiritual values, describing spiritual behaviors, and identifying spiritual people. Follow up with a discussion of spiritual activities, such as meditation and prayer, communing with nature or art, or committing to community service, including what research shows about how they relate to recovery. Ask participants what they think about spiritual activities, whether they practice any in their daily lives, and if they would consider adding any.

Defining Spirituality

It is said that addiction is as much a spiritual disorder as it is a physical and psychosocial one. But this doesn't mean that a substance use disorder is the result of a lack of religiosity in participants' lives, nor does it mean that Twelve Step fellowships are religious organizations that provide the solution for addiction.

Religiosity refers to the degree to which individuals actively participate in an organized religion. Generally speaking, religiosity varies from intense (orthodox) to mild (casual). And while involvement in Twelve Step fellowships can also vary, they are by no means organized religions. Religions the world over are characterized by a written dogma administered by ordained clergy, in turn monitored by a clerical hierarchy that determines the dogma. Twelve Step fellowships have none of these. While fellowship meeting groups may attract members of similar religious beliefs, the program itself refers to "God" with the qualifying phrase *as we understood Him,* ensuring pluralistic fellowships that are open to any religious denomination, as well as agnostics and atheists. In fact, AA's Big Book includes a chapter titled "We Agnostics." The Twelve Steps advocate for letting go of arrogance and self-centeredness in favor of humility and open-mindedness.

Spirituality is different from religiosity. Spirituality has to do with personal values and how personal conduct relates to those values. While we've established that Twelve Step fellowships are not religions, they do clearly advocate for certain values and behaviors, such as honesty, communication, altruism, prayer or meditation, humility, and amends for harm done to others. With this in mind, substance use disorders can be understood as spiritual illnesses because as use progresses (from moderate to severe), individuals typically progressively violate their own moral values and standards of conduct. This leads to a great deal of guilt and shame, which need to be addressed as part of the recovery process. For teens, substance use may arrest the process of spiritual development, leading to the state of ennui discussed earlier.

Spirituality and Recovery

The role of spirituality in recovery has been examined through research in recent years. One researcher found that for one hundred AA members, engaging in spiritual activities such as meditation, prayer, communing with nature, and reading spiritual literature had a positive effect on recovery—above and beyond the positive effects from meeting attendance alone.[1] Another study found that those who reported stronger spiritual beliefs and practices (such as meditating and reading spiritual literature) were more likely to remain abstinent (and were likely to use less in the case of a slip).[2] The positive outcomes associated with this research support the discussion of spiritual beliefs and activities within the TSF and TSF-COD programs.

Meditation and Prayer

Meditation and prayer are integral to Step Eleven and have been part of the Twelve Step approach to recovery since the beginning. Both spiritual activities have the power to relax the body and focus the mind. The positive health benefits associated with meditation, including its impact on stress levels, have been well documented with research. In fact, government institutions such as the National Institutes of Health now share information and advocate for the practice of meditation for certain health conditions.[3] Spiritual activities, meditation in particular, should be an important focus for this topic and make for excellent recovery tasks.

Negative Religious Experiences

Although the majority of men and women express positive feelings toward their religion, this is not universally true. Indeed, some individuals with substance use disorders may have at some point experienced exploitation, rejection, or abuse through their participation in organized religion. Such experiences understandably create skepticism around the role of religion in their lives. Both TSF and TSF-COD emphasize the spiritual nature of the Twelve Steps rather than frame the content in a particular religious context, and this is especially important for participants with negative religious experiences in their past. It is essential that facilitation of the program is respectful of this distinction and does not advocate for any particular religious perspective, regardless of the facilitator's own religious beliefs.

Agnosticism and Atheism

While some people who participate in TSF and TSF-COD will previously have had negative religious experiences, others will identify as either agnostic (the belief that the existence of God is unable to be known) or atheist (the belief that God does not exist). Such beliefs do not preclude embracing the values found in Twelve Step culture (honesty, altruism, humility, and so on) or engaging in activities like meditation and sponsorship that are part of the Twelve Step approach to recovery. Encouraging skeptical participants to "shop around" for meetings they may be more comfortable in can help, as well as emphasizing the adage "Take what works and leave the rest." The correlation between recovery and spirituality should be emphasized with all participants, but agnostic and atheist participants should be encouraged to pursue one value or behavior in order to help facilitate development within the spiritual recovery domain.

Adolescent Considerations

Some argue that the topic of spirituality is not one that teens relate to. We respectfully disagree. Deciding what values one wants to live by is actually an essential element of adolescent development. Such values influence the adolescents' developing sense of identity: What do I stand for, what matters to me, and how will I judge my own behavior and choices moving forward? As mentioned earlier, a state of ennui may describe many teens with substance use disorders. Engaging them in discussions on identity, values, and purpose can be pivotal to recovery. One teen, for example, who often challenged the facilitator in group

TSF sessions responded to the question "How do you think of yourself?" by stating "I challenge people." The facilitator reframed this as "So you like to question authority," but then asked, "What else do you stand for? What else is important to you?" In our experience, the discussion that this TSF topic is intended to facilitate is sure to be lively, and very much relevant to the choices teens make about recovery.

Recovery Tasks

During this session, participants are encouraged to think about one spiritual activity that they would be willing to try out. Participants also commit to attend Twelve Step meetings of their choice. If a participant does not yet have a sponsor, he or she should be encouraged to take steps before the next session to get one. Participants are encouraged to continue their networking efforts. Continued reading of conference-approved Twelve Step fellowship literature is recommended, alongside any other readings suggested by the facilitator. The participant workbooks help with reviewing content, tracking sober days, and analyzing slips.

■ ■ ■

15

Termination

The TSF termination session, like the introductory session, has a unique format. The main goal of this session is to allow the facilitator and participants to process participant experiences in TSF or TSF-COD together. A second goal is to encourage continuing participant involvement in Twelve Step fellowships as their main support in recovery.

Assessing the Experience

Honesty is incredibly important in the evaluation of participant experience with the TSF or TSF-COD program. Different participants find different parts of the program to be helpful. During this session, participants perform a self-examination where they evaluate how the treatment experience may have influenced them. Feedback is good for facilitators, and being open to honest criticism offers a good example for the participant of how to be receptive to feedback—an important element to Twelve Step fellowship support.

This is also a good opportunity to re-administer the Alcoholics Anonymous Affiliation Scale (AAAS) or the Twelve Step Affiliation and Practices Scale (TSAPS) found in reproducible format on the CD-ROM that accompanies each facilitator guide. The results can be compared against those collected in Core Topic 1: Assessment, which offers a measurement of treatment outcomes. This will also encourage ongoing Twelve Step meeting attendance and involvement.

Regardless of participants' degree of success in the program (sober days versus slips), the program should end on a respectful note. Keep in mind that participants with many slips, as well as those in denial, may someday see the light. Perhaps it will come after the next negative consequence, or maybe it won't come until many more negative

consequences have taken their toll. Nonetheless, the information provided in this program could very well sow the seeds for action and
change at some point down the road.

■ ■ ■

PART 4

Twelve Step Facilitation
for Co-occurring Disorders

16

Introduction to TSF-COD

Twelve Step Facilitation for Co-occurring Disorders (TSF-COD) is an adaptation of TSF for individuals diagnosed with both a substance use disorder and a mental health disorder. The TSF-COD program has its origins in a number of empirical findings. Twelve Step recovery is not a cure for a mental health disorder. But there is a clear correlation between substance use disorders and mental health disorders. As a substance use disorder worsens, the likelihood of a co-occurring mental health disorder increases. Subsequently, recovery from a substance use disorder likely facilitates recovery from a mental health disorder.

The data from these studies show that active involvement in and commitment to a Twelve Step fellowship offer therapeutic promise beyond recovery for substance use disorders—providing evidence-based support for the TSF-COD program. There are two primary goals of the TSF-COD program: recovery from substance use disorders and recovery from mental health disorders.

NIAAA National Survey

The National Institute on Alcohol Abuse and Alcoholism (NIAAA) funded a national survey on alcohol use and its relation to mental illness designed to reflect the entire U.S. population. An interview of 20,291 people ages eighteen and older collected data on participants' experiences during the previous year.[1] The interview collected information about how much each individual drank, as well as any known history of a mental health disorder. The researchers were not so much interested in whether the individuals being interviewed were in treatment for either an alcohol use disorder or a mental health disorder, but rather were looking for insight into how many people had

- *both* a mental health disorder and a substance use disorder (co-occurring disorders)
- *either* a mental health disorder or a substance use disorder
- *neither* a mental health disorder nor a substance use disorder

The authors presented their data in terms of the odds of someone having certain mental health disorders as well as either a moderate or severe alcohol use disorder.

Table 3. Relation of Alcohol Use Disorder to Mental Health Disorders

MENTAL HEALTH DISORDER	ODDS: MODERATE ALCOHOL USE DISORDER	ODDS: SEVERE ALCOHOL USE DISORDER
Depression	1.1 to 1	3.9 to 1
Anxiety	1.7 to 1	2.6 to 1
PTSD	1.5 to 1	2.2 to 1
Schizophrenia	1.9 to 1	3.8 to 1

The data show that people with a moderate alcohol use disorder have about equal chances of having suffered from depression in the last year as people with no alcohol use disorder (a 1.1 to 1 ratio). In other words, this level of drinking does not appear to pose a greater-than-average risk for depression. However, people with a severe alcohol use disorder are almost four times as likely to have experienced depression within the past year when compared to those with no alcohol use disorder (3.9 to 1 ratio).

The data also show that people with a moderate alcohol use disorder are almost twice as likely to suffer from an anxiety disorder as those who do not have an alcohol use disorder (1.7 to 1 ratio). Those with a severe alcohol use disorder are more than two-and-a-half times as likely to have an anxiety disorder when compared to those with no alcohol use disorder (2.6 to 1 ratio). Similar outcomes were found with post-traumatic stress disorder (PTSD); those with a moderate alcohol use disorder are one-and-a-half times more likely to have PTSD compared to those without an alcohol use disorder (1.5 to 1 ratio), while those with a severe alcohol use disorder are more than twice as likely to have PTSD. Data associated with schizophrenia show this trend continuing—individuals with a moderate alcohol use disorder are almost twice as likely to have schizophrenia (1.9 to 1 ratio) compared to those who do not have an alcohol use disorder, and those with a severe alcohol use disorder are nearly four times as likely to have schizophrenia.

So does all this data show that drinking causes anxiety, depression, PTSD, and schizophrenia? Probably not, as it does not make sense that drinking alone could cause such a diverse range of mental health disorders. It does suggest several things, however:

- Many men and women (though by no means all) who seek help for an alcohol use disorder are, *in addition*, likely to suffer from some form of mental health disorder.

- The higher the severity of an individual's alcohol use disorder, the more likely it is that he or she also has a co-occurring mental health disorder. It is possible that drinking has made an existing mental health disorder worse, and it's also possible that individuals with a mental health disorder have turned to drinking as a means of self-medicating.

- Men and women with co-occurring disorders may have a more successful recovery if treatment for an alcohol use disorder takes place at the same time as treatment for a mental health disorder.

Twelve Step Fellowships and Co-occurring Disorders

The idea that people with substance use disorders may have initially started use in an effort to relieve symptoms of a mental health disorder merits further exploration. It's also worth exploring how Twelve Step fellowship involvement can help support recovery from mental health disorders. Researcher George Fein looked into the prevalence of psychiatric diagnoses with people in recovery for an alcohol use disorder. Subjects were divided into a short-term abstinent group (abstinent between five and fifteen weeks) and a long-term abstinent group (abstinent between eighteen months and thirty-two years). A one-to-one interview yielded information on whether individuals had no diagnosable mental health disorder or whether at some point in their lives they had bipolar disorder, dysthymia (chronic low-grade depression), major depression, agoraphobia (anxiety associated with open spaces), panic disorder (anxiety associated with panic attacks), post-traumatic stress disorder (which includes symptoms of both depression and anxiety), or social phobia (anxiety associated with interpersonal interactions).[2]

More than 60 percent of the individuals in both the short-term and the long-term abstinent groups reported a diagnosis of either anxiety or depression at some point in their lives, compared to 15 percent among a control group of men and women without an alcohol use disorder. Fein also found no difference between the results of the short-term abstinent group and the long-term abstinent group, indicating in his own words that "such diagnoses do not impact one's ability to achieve or maintain abstinence." Mental health disorders themselves may not constitute a major barrier to recovery, but left untreated, they may hinder recovery efforts.

Another study found that AA and NA meeting attendance was comparable between those in treatment for a substance use disorder and those in treatment for both a substance use disorder and a mental health disorder.[3] The one notable exception was for people with both a substance use disorder and schizophrenia. Schizophrenia is associated with impaired social skills—the very skills required to get active in a Twelve Step fellowship. For these participants, it is helpful to work toward enhancing social skills and reducing social anxiety as much as possible, since this can help make participants more comfortable with getting active in Twelve Step fellowships.

A lot of the men and women with co-occurring disorders who participate in Twelve Step fellowships attest to the benefits of these groups and the social support they offer for someone in recovery. AA cofounder Bill W. was open about his own struggle with chronic depression, consulting with psychiatrists throughout adulthood.[4] Some people, however, feel more comfortable in Twelve Step fellowships that address the unique needs of those with co-occurring disorders.

> To recover, however, a person with a dual diagnosis of alcohol or other drug addiction and mental illness needs

a strong support structure. This means not only AA (or another Twelve Step group) but very likely a mental health support group that addresses the disorder from which the person is suffering.

—*Kate S.*[5]

There are many Twelve Step groups both nationally and internationally that are specifically designed for people with co-occurring disorders. These may include

- Double Trouble in Recovery (DTR)
- Dual Recovery Anonymous (DRA)
- Dual Diagnosis Anonymous (DDA)
- Schizophrenics Anonymous
- Emotions Anonymous (EA)
- Depression and Bipolar Support Alliance (DBSA)

Twelve Step fellowship involvement is an important goal of the TSF-COD program, and there are some considerations that can help determine which fellowships to recommend. Availability is important— where meetings are located, whether a participant can get to those meetings, and so on. It's a good idea to stay up to date on locally available resources, since meeting times and locations continually change. Individual participant barriers are also important. People with mental health disorders may need help feeling more comfortable socially. Here again, therapeutic strategies such as coaching and role-playing can be helpful. For some, attending online meetings may be a prelude to face-to-face involvement. The most important thing is for participants to find meetings where they feel comfortable, and an increasing number of Twelve Step fellowships are accepting of members taking prescribed medications.

Clinical Trials of TSF-COD

Depression

Recent research has focused on how Twelve Step recovery impacts mental health. Researchers studied men and women diagnosed with both a substance use disorder and major depression. One study had all participants receive antidepressants but compared two different treatment approaches: Integrated Cognitive-Behavioral Therapy (ICBT) and Twelve Step Facilitation (TSF).[6] ICBT teaches coping skills and other strategies to both relieve depression and reduce and resist substance use urges. The primary focus of the TSF program is treating participants' substance use disorders. Data were collected at four stages—midway through treatment, at the end of treatment, three months post-treatment, and six months post-treatment. Results of data analysis showed depression scores among those receiving TSF decreased more than the scores among the ICBT group during active treatment. Both groups showed equal responses to depression at the three-month post-treatment mark, however, supporting the efficacy of both treatment approaches.

A second study comparing ICBT and TSF conducted by this same group of researchers yielded some interesting results:

- Greater Twelve Step meeting attendance and involvement showed reduced rates of depression and substance use.

- TSF once again showed significantly lower levels of depression throughout active treatment compared to ICBT.

- Meeting attendance directly correlated with TSF's positive effect on depression.

- Lower depression scores at the three- and six-month marks predicted lower use at the six- and nine-month marks.

A third study of 1,706 men and women diagnosed with a severe alcohol use disorder measured depression, AA meeting attendance, and alcohol use. Post-treatment comparisons showed that greater AA meeting attendance was associated with better subsequent alcohol use outcomes and decreased depression. The researchers concluded, "AA appears to lead both to improvements in alcohol use and psychological and emotional well-being, which, in turn, may reinforce further abstinence and recovery-related change."[7]

PTSD

A study of those with both a substance use disorder and PTSD compared two different therapeutic approaches: TSF and Substance Dependence Post-Traumatic Stress Disorder Therapy (SDPT). While TSF focuses on treatment of substance use disorders through involvement in Twelve Step fellowships, SDPT uses Stress Inoculation Therapy (SIT), systematic desensitization, and cognitive-behavioral approaches, including in vivo exposure therapy. The researchers concluded that other than the SDPT participants attending more therapy sessions than the TSF participants, there were no significant differences in outcomes between treatments.[8]

The overall sample showed improvements in substance use disorders, PTSD severity, and psychiatric severity. What is most striking about these results is not that SDPT and TSF both showed efficacy, but that TSF worked as well for symptoms of PTSD as a treatment program specifically designed with PTSD patients in mind.

■ ■ ■

17

Important Considerations for TSF-COD

Like TSF, TSF-COD is a structured treatment program that allows for flexibility in treatment planning. The program structure and session format are the same as in TSF (see chapter 4 on page 41), but there are additional considerations unique to TSF-COD, such as education on co-occurring disorders, overcoming barriers to effective mental health treatment, adherence to medication, side effects, and the presence or absence of target symptoms. Effective communication between participants and prescribers is encouraged, and some participants may benefit from referrals to additional counseling.

Mental Health Slips

In addition to a slip involving the use of alcohol or other drugs, a "slip" in the TSF-COD program could also involve not taking psychotropic medication as prescribed, such as taking higher dosages than recommended or deciding to skip medications. Slips can sometimes reflect inner ambivalence (e.g., "I'm not really sure I need to take this medication") or a response to outside resistance (e.g., being told, "You're perfectly all right and don't need to take medication"). Other kinds of mental health slips include not keeping an appointment with a prescriber or an assigned case manager, in which case the participant should discuss the slip with his or her prescriber, and intentionally not taking psychotropic medications in anticipation of drinking or using. The same format used in TSF for analyzing slips can also be used in treatment for mental health disorders.

- social context: Where were you? Whom were you with?
- cognitive context: What were you thinking?
- emotional context: What were you feeling?

Some participants may simply forget about an appointment or run out of medication. The response to mental health slips should follow the same format as the response to substance use slips (see chapter 7 on page 79).

Collaborating with Prescribers

When working with participants who have co-occurring disorders, facilitators must be prepared to collaborate with health care or mental health professionals also involved in participants' treatment. It is important for TSF-COD facilitators to communicate with whoever is prescribing and monitoring psychotropic medications, as well as the case managers assigned to each participant. Depending on the availability of medical personnel, as well as participant preferences, a prescriber may be any of the following:

- primary care physician (MD)
- psychiatrist (MD)
- advanced practice registered nurse (APRN) or nurse practitioner (NP)
- physician's assistant (PA)
- psychologist licensed to prescribe psychotropic medications (PhD or PsyD)

In order to work collaboratively with participant prescribers or case managers, a signed release of information (ROI) form will need to be obtained from each participant. The ROI should clearly state that it is being given for the purpose of "coordination of care." A copy should be kept by the TSF-COD facilitator, and the original(s) should be sent to the prescriber and case manager. Care coordination is more easily achieved at locations that integrate mental health and substance use treatment.

Once the ROI is obtained and sent, the TSF-COD facilitator can initiate contact with a participant's prescriber and case manager, briefly explain the nature of the TSF-COD treatment program, answer any questions, and request permission for future contact if any of the following are reported by the participant:

- nonadherence to a prescription medication regimen
- ineffectiveness of prescribed medications
- negative side effects associated with medications

When a participant signs an ROI, it should be made clear that the TSF-COD facilitator will contact the participant's prescriber and case manager in order to work collaboratively and provide integrated care that is in the best interest of the participant. Throughout TSF-COD program facilitation, all involved in participant mental health care are encouraged to establish and maintain open communication.

Recovery Barriers

People who suffer from both a substance use disorder and mental health disorder may encounter barriers to recovery—barriers unique to their situation. Some of the barriers commonly encountered by people are discussed in this chapter. They include

- shame associated with stigma
- ambivalence toward psychiatric treatment
- social anxiety and underdeveloped social skills
- lack of mobility

Shame Associated with Stigma

> The stereotype of the drunk, and the way in which societies have handled public intoxication, seems tame compared to the attitude toward mental illness held by most cultures.
>
> —*The Dual Disorders Recovery Book*[1]

Similar sentiments have been expressed by many individuals with co-occurring disorders. They fear being wrongfully stereotyped as crazy, unpredictable, or even dangerous. As a consequence, many lead a double life, keeping their mental health disorders secret from their AA friends and/or sponsor, but discussing them openly with family, therapists, or significant others. Yet others choose to keep their mental health disorders secret for personal reasons. A woman in recovery for an alcohol use disorder and chronic depression said, "I believe I can usually tell who else in a meeting might be taking medication, but I choose to keep my psychiatric treatment private, and I also don't ask others. I get what I need out of AA without having to disclose my mental illness." Still, the fear of being stigmatized represents a barrier to full disclosure for many with co-occurring disorders, and this is a very appropriate subject for discussion in the TSF-COD program.

Due to ever-expanding and increasingly effective treatments for depression, bipolar disorder, and post-traumatic stress disorder, the stigma around mental health may be lessening in our culture—at least in part. Medication advertisements for these diagnoses are common today. This results in the growing acceptance that mental health disorders are treatable and that no one has any reason to fear someone who has one. Of those in attendance at Twelve Step meetings, it is likely that some are taking medications for things such as anxiety or depression. The fear of being stigmatized may be part of the reason they choose not to disclose this, however.

A related concern for some is that Twelve Step fellowships are opposed to the idea of taking any form of mood-altering drug, even when medically prescribed for a specific mental health disorder. In reality, most Twelve Step fellowships encourage members to follow their doctors' treatment recommendations, including medication for the treatment of a mental health disorder. Regardless, there are members and groups, sometimes referred to as "orthodox," who regard any mood-altering substance as part of the addiction, regardless of the reason. But this barrier is easily overcome by choosing to attend meetings and network with those who welcome medication-assisted treatment.

Ambivalence toward Psychiatric Treatment

Another barrier—one that can present a challenge during program facilitation—is when a participant is ambivalent about psychiatric treatment and/or taking prescribed psychotropic medication. There can be several reasons for this, which need to be explored and worked through in order to facilitate recovery. They include the following:

- **Ambivalence about a mental health diagnosis:** Not everyone is equally accepting of being diagnosed with a mental health disorder. Some may resist taking prescribed medications as part of their ambivalence. Although mental health treatment is not the primary focus of TSF-COD, it may help to include discussion of this barrier during facilitation—which in turn might be shared with mental health practitioners.

- **Social network resistance to mental illness:** The families and friends of some participants may express skepticism that they have mental health disorders or need medication. Program facilitators can be prepared to address this by supporting the opinion of the mental health provider assigned to the participant and suggesting that the participant receive recovery support for both substance use disorders and mental health disorders.

- **Undesirable medication side effects:** Psychotropic medications can sometimes cause undesirable side effects such as headaches, indigestion, or fatigue. Participants may not share such side effects, however, and these side effects may contribute to resistance for taking medication. Program facilitation of TSF-COD can offer a "bridge" between participants and mental health providers. As such, facilitation can help promote recovery through cooperative therapeutic approaches.

Social Anxiety and Underdeveloped Social Skills
A significant number of individuals with chronic mental health disorders also suffer from social anxiety and underdeveloped social skills. This shyness, as some describe it, can act as a barrier for meeting attendance and active participation in Twelve Step fellowships. In fact, even with a clinical diagnosis and the initiation of a medication regimen, participants can still struggle with social skills or social anxiety. Therefore, participants with these barriers can benefit from treatment that includes guidance on how to make social settings more comfortable. These individuals may not have ever developed basic social skills, so significant remediation may be required for successful integration into Twelve Step fellowships. Therapeutic strategies like role-playing and coaching can be particularly useful in this regard. For example, showing participants how to maintain appropriate social distance, how to make eye contact and smile, and how to introduce themselves may

sound basic, but they can be skills that are underdeveloped in some individuals.

Lack of Mobility

When beginning the TSF or TSF-COD program, it is wise at the outset to inquire about possible barriers to participation, along with possible solutions. Common barriers include lack of transportation (or unreliable transportation), child care responsibilities, and conflicting or variable work schedules. Possible solutions include seeking meetings that are geographically close to the participant and checking out meetings that might have child care. A group format expands the possibilities for solutions, including seeking volunteers to bring another participant to a meeting, or perhaps alternating child care responsibilities so that two members can at least attend some TSF sessions and Twelve Step meetings.

■ ■ ■

TSF-COD Treatment Guidelines

TSF and TSF-COD are divided into core and elective topics. In addition, a two-session conjoint program is available (see part 5, beginning on page 179). Both TSF and TSF-COD include a structured termination session. Both programs can be implemented in either a series of individual or group sessions. We recommend that sessions be held weekly or more frequently, depending on the clinical setting, in order to maintain therapeutic "momentum." The TSF-COD core program consists of sessions covering five topics, and the elective program consists of sessions covering an additional five topics.

Core Topics

- Core Topic 1: Assessment
- Core Topic 2: Acceptance
- Core Topic 3: Surrender
- Core Topic 4: Getting Active in Twelve Step Fellowships
- Core Topic 5: Getting Active in Mental Health Treatment

Elective Topics

- Elective Topic 1: Barriers to Getting Active in Twelve Step Fellowships
- Elective Topic 2: Barriers to Mental Health Treatment
- Elective Topic 3: People, Places, and Routines
- Elective Topic 4: Emotions
- Elective Topic 5: Living for Recovery

Core Topic 4: Getting Active in Twelve Step Fellowships and Core Topic 5: Getting Active in Mental Health Treatment are likely to become ongoing themes throughout the TSF-COD program, in which recovery tasks are suggested and followed up on a regular basis. The elective program allows facilitators to customize the treatment plan to meet the needs of a particular participant or group. The elective topics are intended to support and strengthen active involvement in Twelve Step fellowships and mental health treatment. The elective program allows the TSF-COD program to be tailored to address individual or group barriers to recovery. It may take multiple sessions to cover one topic. Elective topics can be incorporated into treatment plans as appropriate and as time permits.

The TSF-COD program is a derivative of the TSF program, and therefore they share many common elements. The content on mental health disorders included in the TSF-COD program is included in this chapter, where material unique to co-occurring disorders is discussed while avoiding repetition of content already outlined within the TSF program.

TSF-COD Core Topics

Core Topic 1: Assessment
This initial session is focused on identifying active substance use disorders in participants, as well as existing mental health disorders. Assessment should take into account a history of substance use and mental health problems, including any prior treatment undergone by the participant. Assessment for the TSF-COD program follows the assessment used in the TSF program (see chapter 6 on pages 65–75), but a strong focus on existing mental health conditions should be included for participants with co-occurring disorders.

In addition to determining severity of substance use through an evaluation of a participant's substance use history, a comprehensive mental health history takes into account previously identified symptoms, prior diagnoses, and treatment regimens administered in the past. In addition to the negative consequences associated with substance use, negative consequences associated with untreated mental health conditions are also examined. Special attention may be placed on discussing the interaction between substance use and symptoms of mental health disorders. For example, you may initiate a discussion by asking a participant, "Do you think your cocaine use contributes to your hallucinations or racing thoughts?" or "Does drinking make your depression worse?" Facilitation also includes discussing how a participant's substance use may affect willingness or ability to adhere to mental health treatment.

Because of the way that substance use disorders and mental health disorders can interact, an increasing number of mental health practitioners are taking the approach of postponing a definitive psychiatric diagnosis until an individual with co-occurring disorders has been abstinent for a period of time. In this case, communication between the facilitator and the mental health practitioner becomes all the more important.

The TSF and TSF-COD programs also recommend measuring the effectiveness of the treatment program. For this task, we recommend the Alcoholics Anonymous Affiliation Scale (AAAS)[1] or the Twelve Step Affiliation and Practices Scale (TSAPS) found in the facilitator guide and on the CD-ROM that accompanies the facilitator guide. The research conducted on Twelve Step fellowships strongly supports a relationship between *involvement* in a fellowship and recovery. That involvement has been found to correlate positively with abstinence and/or reduced substance use.[2] Such involvement includes meeting attendance, but it goes beyond that basic level of involvement.

Core Topic 2: Acceptance

DIMENSION	KEY CONCEPT	CORE PROCESS	MARKERS
Social/ Behavioral	Getting active	Building a support network	• Active participation • Sponsor • Home group • Mental health treatment
Cognitive	Denial	Acceptance and surrender	• Identifying as a person recovering from a co-occurring disorder • Acceptance of abstinence as a personal goal • Acceptance of mental health treatment • Adherence to a prescription regimen
Spiritual	Personal growth	Spiritual awakening	• Moral inventory • Prayer/meditation • Altruism • Spiritual activities

This topic follows the structure of TSF Core Topic 2 (see chapter 7 on pages 77–85) but includes discussion of any failure to take prescribed medications. Facilitation should involve any conference-approved literature obtained by participants, including literature on co-occurring disorders, such as *Double Trouble in Recovery: Basic Guide,* daily meditations, or any other readings they may find useful. Any negative side effects associated with prescribed medications should be addressed, and this information may be appropriate to pass along to prescribers.

Acceptance includes discussing how willpower alone has not proven sufficient in managing a mental health disorder, and this may involve talking through past experiences of participants. Acceptance of both substance use disorders and mental health disorders is the first step in recovery for those with co-occurring disorders.

Core Topic 3: Surrender

DIMENSION	KEY CONCEPT	CORE PROCESS	MARKERS
Social/ Behavioral	Getting active	Building a support network	• Active participation • Sponsor • Home group • Mental health treatment
Cognitive	Denial	Acceptance and surrender	• Identifying as a person recovering from a co-occurring disorder • Acceptance of abstinence as a personal goal • Acceptance of mental health treatment • Adherence to a prescription regimen
Spiritual	Personal growth	Spiritual awakening	• Moral inventory • Prayer/meditation • Altruism • Spiritual activities

The topic of surrender (see chapter 8 on pages 87–96) involves a further discussion about the limits of willpower, the people participants have turned to in the past for support and guidance, and the participants' current willingness to reach out to others in their recovery from co-occurring disorders. Most important, participants should be asked about their willingness to utilize both a Twelve Step fellowship and mental health treatment (it may be helpful to use a scale of one to ten, where one represents the *least* willing and ten represents the *most* willing). Addressing ambivalence about participation in both is critical to recovery for those with co-occurring disorders, and this is therefore a central part of this topic in the TSF-COD program.

Core Topic 4: Getting Active in Twelve Step Fellowships

DIMENSION	KEY CONCEPT	CORE PROCESS	MARKERS
Social/ Behavioral	Getting active	Building a support network	• Active participation • Sponsor • Home group • Mental health treatment
Cognitive	Denial	Acceptance and surrender	• Identifying as a person recovering from a co-occurring disorder • Acceptance of abstinence as a personal goal • Acceptance of mental health treatment • Adherence to a prescription regimen
Spiritual	Personal growth	Spiritual awakening	• Moral inventory • Prayer/meditation • Altruism • Spiritual activities

The TSF-COD program strongly advocates for active participation in a Twelve Step fellowship as a foundation of recovery, but the particular fellowship recommended will be based on many factors. Some participants will feel comfortable attending both traditional Twelve Step meetings and specialized meetings for co-occurring disorders, while others will only feel comfortable attending one or the other. This decision may be influenced by past experiences as well as a participant's level of social functionality.

Core Topic 5: Getting Active in Mental Health Treatment

DIMENSION	KEY CONCEPT	CORE PROCESS	MARKERS
Social/ Behavioral	Getting active	Building a support network	• Active participation • Sponsor • Home group • Mental health treatment
Cognitive	Denial	Acceptance and surrender	• Identifying as a person recovering from a co-occurring disorder • Acceptance of abstinence as a personal goal • Acceptance of mental health treatment • Adherence to a prescription regimen
Spiritual	Personal growth	Spiritual awakening	• Moral inventory • Prayer/meditation • Altruism • Spiritual activities

This topic follows a similar structure to Core Topic 4 (see chapter 9 on pages 97–104) but specifically focuses on getting active in treatment for a mental health disorder, such as taking prescription medications, making and keeping appointments with prescribers and case managers, attending Twelve Step meetings and/or meetings for co-occurring disorders, working with a sponsor, and other ways of getting involved.

Getting active in mental health treatment begins with actively seeking more information about one's mental health. The goal is to align TSF-COD program facilitation with the participant, the case manager, and mental health professionals working with the participant. Comprehensive treatment typically includes individual and/or group therapy along with psychotropic medication. Adherence to this treatment plan generally constitutes "getting active" in mental health treatment.

Similar to a substance use disorder, an untreated mental health disorder can lead to negative consequences in virtually every sphere of life: occupation, home environment, family, relationships, and so on.

Left untreated, mental health disorders can lead to a life that becomes increasingly unmanageable. This topic of the TSF-COD program addresses the diagnoses assigned to participants alongside treatment plans to formulate structure around recovery for co-occurring disorders.

Once again, participants should be asked about their readiness to participate in mental health treatment (similar to Core Topic 3, it may be helpful to use a scale of one to ten, where one represents the *least* willing and ten represents the *most* willing). Scores of five or less should lead to a discussion about ambivalence and participants' reluctance to fully engage in mental health treatment. Use of the participant workbook can be helpful for this activity.

TSF-COD Elective Topics

Elective Topic 1: Barriers to Getting Active in Twelve Step Fellowships

DIMENSION	KEY CONCEPT	CORE PROCESS	MARKERS
Social/ Behavioral	Getting active	Building a support network	• Active participation • Sponsor • Home group • Mental health treatment
Cognitive	Denial	Acceptance and surrender	• Identifying as a person recovering from a co-occurring disorder • Acceptance of abstinence as a personal goal • Acceptance of mental health treatment • Adherence to a prescription regimen
Spiritual	Personal growth	Spiritual awakening	• Moral inventory • Prayer/meditation • Altruism • Spiritual activities

There are common barriers to involvement in Twelve Step fellowship meetings among those with co-occurring disorders. Participants may have social anxiety, which can present a significant therapeutic challenge and cause ambivalence about attending meetings. Because of this, facilitation of this topic may span multiple sessions. Role-playing exercises can be helpful, with themes such as easing anxiety in social scenarios, maintaining personal space, making eye contact, and introducing oneself to others. In fact, these exercises can be extended by having participants imagine these role-playing scenarios when they are alone at home or they can practice them again with others. Facilitators also may want to consider additional recovery barriers unique to participants with co-occurring disorders (see pages 159–62 in chapter 17).

Group facilitation of TSF-COD can actually be beneficial for those with social anxiety, as it can help participants become more comfortable with attending Twelve Step fellowship meetings. For example, participants may be encouraged to attend meetings together and report back to the group during the following session. As group facilitation of the TSF-COD program continues, the reality of becoming more comfortable in group settings sets the stage for fellowship meetings. Other common barriers to active involvement for participants with co-occurring disorders may include the following:

- Ambivalence about loss of control: Participants may be reluctant to accept the severity of their substance use disorder, but presenting objective facts about consequences linked to substance use and discussing past failed attempts to moderate or stop use can prove helpful to this topic. When working in a group format, encourage members to share their own past experiences with trying to stop or moderate, and what the results were.

- Lifestyle complications: Lack of transportation and difficulty obtaining child care are common problems, but facilitators can assist with finding meetings that offer child care and volunteers that may be able to assist with transportation.

- Network support for substance use: Social networks that support substance use can make the difficult first steps toward recovery even more difficult, but TSF-COD facilitation can help participants see how Twelve Step fellowships offer an alternative social network that supports recovery instead. Role-playing how to tell a skeptical friend or family member that the participant has decided to attend AA is also an effective strategy.

Elective Topic 2: Barriers to Mental Health Treatment

DIMENSION	KEY CONCEPT	CORE PROCESS	MARKERS
Social/ Behavioral	Getting active	Building a support network	• Active participation • Sponsor • Home group • Mental health treatment
Cognitive	Denial	Acceptance and surrender	• Identifying as a person recovering from a co-occurring disorder • Acceptance of abstinence as a personal goal • Acceptance of mental health treatment • Adherence to a prescription regimen
Spiritual	Personal growth	Spiritual awakening	• Moral inventory • Prayer/meditation • Altruism • Spiritual activities

There are also common barriers that stand in the way of active participation in mental health treatment. Special considerations for co-occurring disorders can be helpful with facilitation of this topic (see pages 160–61 in chapter 17). It is recommended that this elective topic be incorporated into a treatment plan for all participants who show patterns of nonadherence to medications, and this may need to be addressed in more than one session. Role-playing may be appropriate for some, with a theme such as how to tell a prescriber about the negative side effects experienced with psychotropic medication.

Again, group facilitation can actually be a benefit for this topic, since it is likely that group members will be struggling with some of the same issues. Discussing these barriers in an open, frank, nonjudgmental manner can assist others with recovery efforts. Some of the common mental health barriers for participants with co-occurring disorders include the following:

- Ambivalence about mental health diagnoses: Some participants may have difficulty accepting that they have a mental health disorder, especially when it requires taking medication.

- Unsupportive social networks: Some individuals have social networks that do not support the diagnosis of mental health disorders or the need for treatment.

- Side effects of medications: Participants may experience undesirable side effects that they will often fail to report to a prescriber or a case manager.

- Self-medication: Some participants will likely have attempted to substitute alcohol and other drugs for prescribed psychotropic medication. Discuss these efforts and their outcomes.

Elective Topic 3: People, Places, and Routines

DIMENSION	KEY CONCEPT	CORE PROCESS	MARKERS
Social/ Behavioral	Getting active	Building a support network	• Active participation • Sponsor • Home group • Mental health treatment
Cognitive	Denial	Acceptance and surrender	• Identifying as a person recovering from a co-occurring disorder • Acceptance of abstinence as a personal goal • Acceptance of mental health treatment • Adherence to a prescription regimen
Spiritual	Personal growth	Spiritual awakening	• Moral inventory • Prayer/meditation • Altruism • Spiritual activities

Recovery from a substance use disorder and concurrent treatment for a mental health disorder require a commitment to significant lifestyle changes. Routines often play an important role, since rituals and habits can trigger substance use. Part of recovery involves replacing a social network and lifestyle that supports substance use with one that supports sobriety (see chapter 12 on pages 119–27), and this same approach can equally be applied to recovery from a mental health disorder.

Participants with co-occurring disorders will need to learn to avoid individuals who do not acknowledge a mental health disorder or do not support their need for psychotropic medication or mental health treatment. Specialized Twelve Step fellowships for those with co-occurring disorders offer support for those in recovery. Where these fellowships are not locally available, a TSF-COD facilitator (or other members of a TSF group) may offer support, as can prescribers and case managers.

Elective Topic 4: Emotions

DIMENSION	KEY CONCEPT	CORE PROCESS	MARKERS
Social/ Behavioral	Getting active	Building a support network	• Active participation • Sponsor • Home group • Mental health treatment
Cognitive	Denial	Acceptance and surrender	• Identifying as a person recovering from a co-occurring disorder • Acceptance of abstinence as a personal goal • Acceptance of mental health treatment • Adherence to a prescription regimen
Spiritual	Personal growth	Spiritual awakening	• Moral inventory • Prayer/meditation • Altruism • Spiritual activities

For any recovering participant, managing difficult emotions can have larger therapeutic implications than simply how those emotions relate to substance use (see chapter 13, pages 129–37). But for those with co-occurring disorders, difficult emotions may also relate to a mental health disorder. This topic seeks to identify emotional triggers most dangerous to recovery and to think of ways to deal with these emotions without substance use.

The AA publication *Living Sober* discusses how feeling hungry, angry, lonely, or tired (HALT) commonly triggers slips or relapses for those with substance use disorders. Alternatives include going to a meeting; calling, texting, or emailing a recovering friend or sponsor; or talking to a prescriber, therapist, or case manager if the trigger is related to a mental health disorder, such as depression or PTSD. Introducing HALT appeals to the collective wisdom of Twelve Step fellowships to provide a working example of how to address both physical states (hungry, tired) and emotional states (angry, lonely) before they trigger a slip.

Other potent trigger emotions that warrant consideration include

• loneliness and isolation

• unresolved and lingering resentments

• boredom and ennui (especially among adolescents)

• guilt

• shame

• grief

Elective Topic 5: Living for Recovery

DIMENSION	KEY CONCEPT	CORE PROCESS	MARKERS
Social/ Behavioral	Getting active	Building a support network	• Active participation • Sponsor • Home group • Mental health treatment
Cognitive	Denial	Acceptance and surrender	• Identifying as a person recovering from a co-occurring disorder • Acceptance of abstinence as a personal goal • Acceptance of mental health treatment • Adherence to a prescription regimen
Spiritual	Personal growth	Spiritual awakening	• Moral inventory • Prayer/meditation • Altruism • Spiritual activities

Many with a long history of severe substance use and a co-occurring mental health disorder have experienced a deterioration of lifestyle as a consequence. This topic is intended to assist participants in learning how to build and sustain a healthy lifestyle. The HALT material in Elective Topic 4 discussed how to respond to physical and emotional states, and this topic examines nutrition, eating habits, exercise or physical conditioning, and hobbies or other interests. This may be a particular concern for those who suffer from the most chronic and severe mental health disorders, such as schizophrenia, schizoaffective disorder, severe recurrent depression, or severe bipolar disorder. Even with concurrent mental health treatment, coaching on healthy lifestyle management can prove beneficial, as many participants may live very dysfunctional lifestyles. Some agencies provide day centers where participants can spend time socializing, learning skills (e.g., job interviewing), and even getting a healthy meal.

Participants benefit by reviewing their own lifestyles and setting goals for healthy improvement. Changes in any and all of these areas may be incremental, and that can allow participants to recognize progress and continue monitoring it on their own. Lifestyle changes supportive of recovery are discussed and examined, such as exercising regularly to augment the effectiveness of antidepressant medications, changing eating habits from one large meal a day (or no meals at all) to eating three smaller meals, and getting someone with chronic schizophrenia who is socially isolated to agree to visit a community health drop-in center twice a week. This topic includes a brief overview of spirituality. Lifestyle changes represent significant progress in building a healthier lifestyle and can go a long way toward supporting recovery.

Termination

The final TSF-COD session asks participants to examine their own beliefs about mental health disorders and addiction, discuss their experience with TSF-COD, and outline plans for the immediate future. (See chapter 15 on pages 145–46 for information about the Termination session.) The emphasis is, of course, on plans that support recovery for co-occurring disorders. This includes continued support from Twelve Step fellowships, therapists, prescribers, case managers, and others.

This is also a good opportunity to re-administer the Alcoholics Anonymous Affiliation Scale (AAAS) or the Twelve Step Affiliation and Practices Scale (TSAPS), available in reproducible format on the CD-ROM that accompanies the facilitator guide. The results can be compared against those collected in Core Topic 1: Assessment, which offers a measurement of treatment outcomes. This will also encourage ongoing Twelve Step meeting attendance and involvement.

■ ■ ■

PART 5

Conjoint Program

>>

Conjoint Program

The conjoint program provides two topics for the participant and a significant other to take part in together. A significant other could be anyone the participant feels (a) plays an important role in his or her life, (b) is supportive of recovery, and (c) is in frequent contact. Permission for the facilitator to contact the significant other should be given by the participant. Include the conjoint program whenever possible, as it can strongly support participant recovery with both substance use disorders and mental health disorders.

There are three main learning objectives associated with the conjoint program: to identify the significant other's level of substance use (a potentially risky influence), to discuss enabling and caring detachment, and to practice caring detachment rather than enabling. Significant others who themselves have even a mild substance use disorder are not appropriate for the conjoint program. Adolescents who participate will need permission from a legal guardian.

■ ■ ■

Conjoint Topic 1: Enabling

The conjoint program begins with an overview of the TSF program, including its encouragement of Twelve Step fellowship involvement. The following points are made in the overview of the program:

- Substance use disorders affect the body, mind, and spirit; are characterized by loss of control and obsession with use; and are progressive—they usually lead to predictable consequences and predictable symptoms.

- There is no "cure" for substance use disorders, but involvement in Twelve Step fellowships has proven effective in managing recovery with substance use disorders (and involvement with mental health treatment is effective for managing mental health disorders).

- Though it may take many forms, those with severe substance use disorders frequently experience denial—they resist accepting that they have lost the ability to effectively stop or control their use ("I can control my use," "What happened last time won't happen again," and so on). Those with co-occurring disorders may also try to convince themselves and others that they do not need mental health treatment.

- Slips (substance use after a period of abstinence and refusals to adhere to psychotropic medications) are unfortunate but understandable, although it is vital that those with substance use disorders and co-occurring mental health disorders respond to urges or slips appropriately, such as by going to a Twelve Step meeting, calling a Twelve Step fellowship friend or sponsor, or discussing the slip with a mental health professional.

The purpose of this conjoint program is to enlist the help of the significant other as a nonprofessional aide in promoting and encouraging recovery from substance use disorders (or from co-occurring disorders).

Potential Barriers

The conjoint topics cover a lot of material related to how the relationship between the participant and the significant other has been affected by the participant's substance use disorder (and possibly co-occurring disorder). Because of this, it is important to stay focused on the topics related to the program, because these sessions are not intended to focus on relationship counseling.

Not all participants will be open to the conjoint program. Some will be outwardly opposed, in fact. Past participants have suggested the conjoint program may make significant others feel guilty, or at least partly responsible, for their substance use disorder. That may sound noble, but the problem with arguments like "This is my problem" or "She's been through enough" is that they assume it is possible to be in a relationship with someone who has a severe substance use disorder (and perhaps a co-occurring disorder as well) and yet be unaffected by it. Put that way, participants may feel less anxiety about trying out conjoint sessions. Other participants may feel guilty themselves or fear blame and possible retribution from a significant other. Some may be in strained relationships or be alienated from significant others. Still others may wish to persist in trying to control significant others, and will therefore avoid discussions on enabling.

Codependency can follow the same predictable course as addiction. Most enablers initially react to a substance use disorder with concern and a desire to help, but as time goes by, and problems get worse instead of better, concern and anxiety give way to frustration and anger and eventually resentment and alienation. Strong feelings from a significant other are understandable and may sensibly result in being skeptical or cynical of recovery. Resentment against the participant, the facilitator, and even the program itself may come up in the conjoint sessions since many significant others may feel that this is "just another ride on the merry-go-round." Such feelings should be validated, as not doing so will likely undermine the facilitator's credibility. But responding to those feelings should include the rationale that two sessions certainly can't hurt, and could even help, the relationship.

It is important to discuss the history and frequency of substance use by the significant other early in the first conjoint session. Significant others who are in recovery themselves (and preferably have a home meeting and sponsor) are good matches for this program. Those in recovery from co-occurring disorders are also good candidates for participation. But significant others who may be at risk for problematic substance use should be encouraged to pursue a diagnostic assessment before participating in a conjoint session. Significant others who themselves have even a mild substance use disorder are not appropriate for the conjoint program.

Enabling

As people progress from a mild substance use disorder to one that is moderate and eventually severe, the people around them are also inevitably affected. And the closer someone is to the one with the substance use disorder, the more likely that person will be affected. Out of concern, they end up taking too much responsibility for the one with the substance use disorder. Close friends and family members may make unsuccessful attempts to manipulate and control their loved one in an effort to get him or her to quit. However, most of these actions end up enabling the one with the substance use disorder.

Enabling means helping the one with a substance use disorder to minimize or avoid the negative consequences associated with use. Enabling can also involve behavior that supports *not* treating a mental health disorder. Some examples include covering up for the individual when he or she is using and might otherwise get into trouble, allowing him or her "a little bit" in the hope that he or she will be satisfied with that, purchasing or lending money for alcohol or other drugs, excusing hostility or abuse that results from substance use or untreated mental health disorders, overlooking self-abuse that stems from untreated mental health disorders such as depression, and defending his or her inappropriate or irresponsible behavior.

These things might make significant others feel as though they are helping, but in actuality they are often helping the one with the substance use disorder to continue using. People don't enable because they want a loved one to keep using or avoid treating a mental health disorder. On the contrary, enabling usually starts and is motivated by an interest in doing "damage control." However, by cushioning the one with the substance use disorder (and co-occurring disorder), the user does not experience the negative consequences associated with ongoing use. Loved ones feel guilty letting the user face the consequences of his or her actions, but it is the truly caring thing to do. Enabling is an unhealthy response to a substance use disorder, but caring detachment represents a healthier response and will be covered in the next topic (see chapter 20, beginning on page 187).

Enabling can become compulsive and cyclical, leaving loved ones such as significant others to obsess over the behavior of the one with a substance use disorder. This is referred to as codependency, and it can also occur with those who have untreated mental health disorders. During this conjoint session, significant others examine codependency in their own relationships and discuss how minimizing the consequences of use (and perhaps an untreated co-occurring disorder) ends up continuing the pattern. Significant others take inventory of ways they have enabled the relationship (and untreated mental health disorder). If necessary, the participant with a substance use disorder (and untreated mental health disorder) can be prompted to provide some examples—this encourages him or her to understand how enabling has been operative in the relationship. Additionally, it will move the relationship away from enabling and toward caring detachment.

Discussing enabling may cause significant others to feel guilty, especially if they don't feel as though their good intentions have been validated. For example, some may say, "I enable because I don't want her to get into trouble," "I'm afraid that I'll lose him if I don't enable," "I'm confused and don't know what else to do," or "It seems cruel not to help." During the enabling inventory exercise, it is helpful to include a discussion about the motivations behind enabling behavior. This can help reveal important emotions the significant other experiences while enabling, such as caring, concern, commitment, and even fear. For many, this will help reduce the stigma often associated with enabling and will enhance motivation to try caring detachment instead.

Addiction and enabling are complementary processes. Those with severe substance use disorders usually actively encourage enabling since it helps them continue substance use. Individuals with untreated mental health disorders often act similarly, wanting others to "pretend" that nothing is wrong. During the enabling inventory, it is also helpful to discuss how the participant has either encouraged (or coerced) the significant other's enabling. The most common forms of this are appeals to anxiety, guilt, or sympathy:

- *Anxiety:* "If you don't help out (or cover up), something terrible will happen to me, you, or both of us."

- *Guilt:* "It's your fault that I have this problem, so you owe it to me to cover up for me." Or: "You should cover up for me (or pretend) out of loyalty."

- *Sympathy:* "I know I've got a problem, but I'm not ready to deal with it yet."

Participating significant others should be encouraged to try out Al-Anon, Nar-Anon, or Co-Dependents Anonymous, where they can listen to others and talk if they wish, and perhaps seek support. Trying it out does not mean making a long-term commitment to attend Al-Anon, Nar-Anon, or Co-Dependents Anonymous meetings, but it certainly can't hurt. Attending even a single meeting might be enough to give the significant other a sense of what these fellowships have to offer. Facilitators may help significant others locate convenient Al-Anon, Nar-Anon, or Co-Dependents Anonymous meetings.

■ ■ ■

20

Conjoint Topic 2: Caring Detachment

Whereas the first conjoint topic examined the role of enabling within the relationship, the second conjoint topic focuses on caring detachment—something the significant other can do to help. Caring detachment means allowing the person with a substance use disorder to deal with the negative consequences of his or her use without interfering. It means realizing that the one with the substance use disorder is an individual who makes his or her own choices, and that includes dealing with the outcomes of those choices. The same is true with people who have untreated mental health disorders.

Caring detachment represents a new dynamic and may take some getting used to, but it is not punishment—rather, it is allowing the one with the substance use disorder to manage his or her own responsibilities. Helping to manage the consequences of someone else's addiction (and untreated co-occurring disorder) doesn't really help the addiction; it usually does the opposite—and it probably doesn't help the relationship, either.

The first goal of this conjoint topic is to define and illustrate examples of caring detachment using examples from the participants' own experiences together. The next goal is to identify ways to practice caring detachment in the relationship going forward. In order to practice caring detachment, the significant other will need to accept powerlessness over addiction and over the one with a substance use disorder. This is not an easy task, but it can be supported by fellowships such as Al-Anon, Nar-Anon, and Co-Dependents Anonymous, as well as the conference-approved literature they publish.

There is a lot of material to be covered in this topic. Answering questions is important, but it is helpful to limit this discussion to allow sufficient time to cover the material on caring detachment.

Potential Barriers

The significant other may experience some of the same barriers to recovery as participants in the TSF-COD program, such as stigma and shame, social anxiety, and lack of mobility (see pages 159–62 in chapter 17). It may be helpful to discuss these barriers openly and to discuss ways to overcome those barriers.

There are many barriers to detachment, such as the belief that caring for someone means taking responsibility for that person, the belief that it is somehow uncaring or cruel to allow a person with a substance use disorder to experience negative consequences of use, and the belief that through personal willpower it is possible to control or change another person. Holding on to the (sometimes unconscious) belief that one person's willpower can substitute for another's may be the most stubborn form of resistance to caring detachment. A frank and respectful dialogue may be necessary to help a reluctant significant other put his or her own beliefs in perspective and set the stage for learning to "Live and let live." This includes letting go of guilt and misplaced caring.

Significant others may express reservations about participating in Al-Anon or a similar fellowship. There's no harm in simply trying it out, and that is the point to keep making. When a significant other continues to have reservations, it may help to explore why he or she is unwilling to try just once. Some frequently asked questions about Al-Anon, Nar-Anon, and Co-Dependents Anonymous include the following:

Q: *What kind of people will I find in these fellowships?*

A: All kinds of people—but you'll all have a relationship with someone who has a substance use disorder, and you've all been affected by that.

Q: *What will I be expected to do?*

A: There are no requirements to do anything. People can just go and listen to see if listening to others in similar situations is helpful in any way. Talking and networking after the meeting can offer additional support, if desired.

Q: *What's the benefit of fellowships like Al-Anon, Nar-Anon, and Co-Dependents Anonymous?*

A: The one with a substance use disorder is not the only one whose life is out of control. Over time, the lives of those involved with them get out of control too. Significant others often experience stress, depression, and frustration. Al-Anon, Nar-Anon, and Co-Dependents Anonymous are sources of support for men and women who find themselves confronted with addiction in similar situations. These fellowships offer a place to start taking care of yourself instead of trying to control someone else.

Q: *What will I be committing myself to?*

A: Nothing. Trying out Al-Anon, Nar-Anon, and Co-Dependents Anonymous with no commitments is just fine.

Detachment

In discussing what detachment is, it can be helpful to start by addressing what it is not. Caring detachment does not mean detaching from the loved one with a substance use disorder or detaching from emotions. Detachment is not feeling obligated to shoulder anyone else's responsibilities, but instead to achieve self-awareness on individual responsibilities—the ones that can be controlled.

> Detaching does not mean we don't care. It means we learn to love, care, and be involved without going crazy. We stop creating all this chaos in our minds and environments. When we are not anxiously and compulsively thrashing about, we become able to make good decisions about how to love people, and how to solve our problems. We become free to care and to love in ways that help others and don't hurt ourselves.
>
> —*Codependent No More*[1]

The motivations behind the enabling behaviors of significant others can be a good way to address the guilt that many of them feel. Despite good intentions, enabling hasn't worked for them. It can be helpful to propose a few hypothetical questions about a situation where the tables are turned:

- Would significant others want someone else taking responsibility for their actions?
- Is that how the significant others handle other friendships?
- Do they think that is a good attitude for parents to take with their children?

An exercise comparing enabling and caring detachment has the participant and the significant other suggest two situations involving consequences related to substance use. It is helpful for them to use experiences from their own recent past when possible, but examples can be offered if they cannot come up with any on their own. In that instance, the facilitator can try offering one example and encouraging them to think of a second real-life situation they recently experienced. If they are still unable to provide an example of their own, another example of a situation can be offered. After coming up with two situations, the participant and the significant other first illustrate an enabling response for both scenarios and then illustrate a response with caring detachment for both.

For instance, take a situation where a woman with a moderate alcohol use disorder wakes up hungover and leaves an hour late for work as a consequence. This is the third time she has done this in as many weeks. Worried that she will face discipline or a poor performance evaluation, she asks her partner to call in for her and say that she has been ill (again), explaining why she will be late to work. An enabling response to this scenario would include the significant other doing this "favor" and helping the woman to avoid the negative consequences. In contrast, a response with caring detachment would include declining the request and allowing the woman to manage the situation on her own, including any consequences that come as a result. A frank reply might be: "I love you, but I'm also concerned about your drinking, and doing this 'favor' is not really going to help you in the long run."

While the example offered seems straightforward, the exercise raises anxiety for both participants and significant others around outcomes, such as what will happen if the woman loses her job, and how will the outcome impact the relationship—could it be jeopardized? Caring detachment requires courage to break away from enabling behavior, and it also requires faith that detaching is ultimately the right thing to do. This exercise may prove challenging for the participant and significant other, but it starts a necessary conversation around responsibilities, boundaries, and the emotional impact of codependence.

> Detachment is many different things . . . It is a gradual discovery of the truth about the family disease . . . It is the process of learning to see things objectively. . . . And it is learning at last to act in your own best interest—what's good for *you*—instead of constantly reacting to whatever the [one with the substance use disorder] does.
>
> —*Detachment and Enabling*[2]

Learning to let go is a process, and fellowships like Al-Anon, Nar-Anon, and Co-Dependents Anonymous are a good source of support throughout that process. Participants may want help selecting meetings that seem most appropriate for them. The skeptical, ambivalent, or shy significant other should be encouraged to simply "go and listen" at a meeting.

It is not uncommon for a participant to resist the idea of a significant other becoming involved with fellowships like Al-Anon, Nar-Anon, and Co-Dependents Anonymous. To the participants, involvement of their significant others in support fellowships often represents the potential loss of a prime enabler—and this can arouse a great deal of anxiety and resistance. The resistance may be obvious, or it may be subtle. For example, telling the facilitator that a significant other "is okay and doesn't need anyone else's help" exemplifies how a participant might speak on behalf of his or her significant other, and how a response might imply that trying out Al-Anon is akin to admitting weakness. Another example is "supporting" a significant other's hesitation by suggesting that he or she is too busy to find and attend a Nar-Anon (or a similar fellowship) meeting.

Returning to the reciprocal process of enabling can help counter this resistance, such as engaging in discussion about how the significant other is feeling, particularly if those emotions have led to enabling behavior in the past. Equally important is acknowledging the ways the participant actively promotes enabling behavior for his or her own self-interests. This offers an opportunity to discuss resistance and can highlight codependency in the relationship.

Significant others should be encouraged to read literature from Al-Anon, Nar-Anon, or Co-Dependents Anonymous, and they should also be encouraged to attend a fellowship meeting. After all, it certainly can't hurt. It may also help to have significant others try out individual counseling (preferably with a professional who has experience working with addiction and is comfortable discussing enabling and caring detachment).

Table 4. Twelve Step Literature for Significant Others

ORGANIZATION	LITERATURE
Al-Anon	*How Al-Anon Works for Families & Friends of Alcoholics* *One Day at a Time in Al-Anon* *Courage to Change*
Nar-Anon	*Thirty-One Days in Nar-Anon*
Co-Dependents Anonymous	*Co-Dependents Anonymous* ("CoDA Book")

■ ■ ■

Notes

Chapter 1: Introduction

1. D. J. Anderson, J. P. McGovern, and R. L. DuPont, "The Origins of the Minnesota Model of Addiction Treatment—A First Person Account," *Journal of Addictive Diseases* 18, no. 1 (1999): 107–14.

2. *Alcoholics Anonymous*, 4th ed. (New York: Alcoholics Anonymous World Services, 2001), 59–60.

3. Institute of Medicine, *Prevention and Treatment of Alcohol Problems: Research Opportunities* (Washington, D.C.: National Academy Press, 1989).

4. K. Humphreys, S. Wing, D. McCarty, J. Chappel, L. Gallant, B. Haberle, T. Horvath, L. A. Kaskutas, T. Kirk, D. Kivlahan, A. Laudet, B. S. McCrady, A. T. McClellan, J. Morgenstern, M. Townsend, and R. Weiss, "Self-Help Organizations for Alcohol and Drug Problems: Toward Evidence-Based Practice and Policy," *Journal of Substance Abuse Treatment* 26 (2004): 151–58.

5. Project MATCH Research Group, "Matching Alcoholism Treatments to Client Heterogeneity: Project MATCH Posttreatment Drinking Outcomes," *Journal of Studies on Alcoholism* 58, no. 1 (1997): 7–29; Project MATCH Research Group, "Matching Alcoholism Treatments to Client Heterogeneity: Project MATCH Three-Year Drinking Outcomes," *Alcoholism: Clinical and Experimental Research* 22, no. 6 (1998): 1300–1311.

6. W. R. Miller, "Are Alcoholism Treatments Effective? The Project MATCH Data: Response," *BMC Public Health* 5 (2005): 76.

7. K. S. Walitzer, K. H. Dermen, and C. Barrick, "Facilitating Involvement in Alcoholics Anonymous During Out-Patient Treatment—A Randomized Clinical Trial," *Addiction* 104, no. 3 (2009): 391–401; K. Humphreys and R. Moos, "Can Encouraging Substance Abuse Patients to Participate in Self-Help Groups Reduce Demand for Health Care? A Quasi-Experimental Study," *Alcoholism: Clinical and Experimental Research* 25, no. 5 (2001): 711–16; M. D. Litt, R. M. Kadden, E. Kabela-Cormier, and N. M. Petry, "Changing Network Support for Drinking: Network Support Project 2-Year Follow-Up," *Journal of Consulting and Clinical Psychology* 77, no. 2 (2009): 229–42.

8. J. F. Kelly and G. Beresin, "In Defense of 12 Steps: What Science Really Tells Us About Addiction," April 7, 2014, www.wbur.org/commonhealth/2014/04/07/defense-12-step-addiction#comment-1324673907.

9. K. Humphreys and R. Moos, "Can Encouraging Substance Abuse Patients to Participate in Self-Help Groups Reduce Demand for Health Care? A Quasi-Experimental Study," *Alcoholism: Clinical and Experimental Research* 25, no. 5 (2001): 711–16.

10. *Alcoholics Anonymous*, 4th ed. (New York: Alcoholics Anonymous World Services, 2001), 58.

Chapter 2: Important Considerations

1. For assistance in ordering the BHI-MV, contact a behavioral health sales representative at www.hazelden.org/web/public/pub_outreachsales.page.

2. *Narcotics Anonymous,* 6th ed. (Van Nuys, CA: Narcotics Anonymous World Services, 2008), 8.

3. *Alcoholics Anonymous,* 4th ed. (New York: Alcoholics Anonymous World Services, 2001), 30.

4. *Narcotics Anonymous,* 6th ed. (Van Nuys, CA: Narcotics Anonymous World Services, 2008), 7.

5. Ibid., 14–15.

6. *Alcoholics Anonymous,* 4th ed. (New York: Alcoholics Anonymous World Services, 2001), 22–23.

7. *Narcotics Anonymous,* 6th ed. (Van Nuys, CA: Narcotics Anonymous World Services, 2008), 14.

8. Ibid., 275–76.

9. *Twelve Steps and Twelve Traditions* (New York: Alcoholics Anonymous World Services, 1981), 130.

10. Ibid., 133–34.

11. Ibid., 132.

12. *Narcotics Anonymous,* 6th ed. (Van Nuys, CA: Narcotics Anonymous World Services, 2008), 273.

13. *Alcoholics Anonymous,* 4th ed. (New York: Alcoholics Anonymous World Services, 2001), 60.

14. D. J. Anderson, *Perspectives on Treatment: The Minnesota Experience* (Center City, MN: Hazelden Publishing, 1981), 20.

15. S. S. O'Malley, A. J. Jaffe, G. Change, S. Rode, R. Schottenfeld, R. E. Meyer, and B. Rounsaville, "Six-Month Follow-Up of Naltrexone and Psychotherapy for Alcohol Dependence," *Archives of General Psychiatry* 53, no. 2 (1996): 217–24; R. D. Weiss, J. S. Potter, D. A. Fiellin, M. Byrne, H. S. Connery, W. Dickinson, J. Gardin, M. L. Griffin, M. N. Gourevitch, D. L. Haller, A. L. Hasson, Z. Huang, P. Jacobs, A. S. Kosinski, R. Lindblad, E. F. McCance-Katz, S. E. Provost, J. Selzer, E. C. Somoza, S. C. Sonne, and W. Ling, "Adjunctive Counseling During Brief and Extended Buprenorphine-Naloxone Treatment for Prescription Opioid Dependence: A 2-Phase Randomized Controlled Trial," *Archives of General Psychiatry* 68, no. 12 (2011): 1238–46.

16. R. D. Weiss, W. B. Jaffee, V. P. de Menil, and C. B. Cogley, "Group Therapy for Substance Use Disorders: What Do We Know?" *Harvard Review of Psychiatry* 12, no. 6 (2004): 339–50.

Chapter 3: Recovery Dimensions

1. R. Longabaugh, P. W. Wirtz, A. Zweben, and R. L. Stout, "Network Support for Drinking, Alcoholics Anonymous, and Long-Term Matching Effects," *Addiction* 93, no. 9 (1998): 1313–33; J. Wu and K. Witkiewitz, "Network Support for Drinking: An Application of Multiple Groups Growth Mixture Modeling to Examine Client-Treatment Matching," *Journal of Studies on Alcohol and Drugs* 69 (2008): 21–29; M. D. Litt, R. M. Kadden, E. Kabela-Cormier, and N. M. Petry, "Changing Network Support for Drinking: Network Support Project 2-Year Follow-Up," *Journal of Consulting and Clinical Psychology* 77, no. 2 (2009): 229–42.

2. *Alcoholics Anonymous 2014 Membership Survey,* www.aa.org/assets/en_US/p-48_membershipsurvey.pdf.

3. L. A. Kaskutas, L. Ammon, K. Delucchi, R. Room, J. Bond, and C. Weisner, "Alcoholics Anonymous Careers: Patterns of AA Involvement Five Years after Treatment Entry," *Alcoholism: Clinical and Experimental Research* 29, no. 11 (2005): 1983–90; J. Witbrodt, Y. Ye, J. Bond, F. Chi, C. Weisner, and J. Mertens, "Alcohol and Drug Treatment Involvement, 12-Step Attendance and Abstinence: 9-Year Cross-Lagged Analysis of Adults in an Integrated Health Plan," *Journal of Substance Abuse Treatment* 46, no. 4 (2014): 412–19.

4. J. Witbrodt, L. Kaskutas, J. Bond, and K. Delucchi, "Does Sponsorship Improve Outcomes Above Alcoholics Anonymous Attendance? A Latent Class Growth Curve Analysis," *Addiction* 107, no. 2 (2012): 301–11.

5. *The A.A. Group . . . Where It All Begins* (New York: Alcoholics Anonymous World Services, 2005), 15.

6. H. M. Tiebout, "Surrender Versus Compliance in Therapy," *Quarterly Journal of Studies on Alcohol* 14 (1953): 58–68.

7. S. A. Buckingham, D. Frings, and I. P. Albery, "Group Membership and Social Identity in Addiction Recovery," *Psychology of Addictive Behaviors* 27, no. 4 (2013): 1132–40.

8. J. F. Kelly, R. L. Stout, M. Magill, J. S. Tonigan, and M. E. Pagano, "Mechanisms of Behavior Change in Alcoholics Anonymous: Does Alcoholics Anonymous Lead to Better Alcohol Use Outcomes by Reducing Depression Symptoms?" *Addiction* 105 (2010): 626–36.

Chapter 4: Structure and Format

1. R. D. Weiss, W. B. Jaffee, V. de Menil, and C. B. Cogley, "Group Therapy for Substance Use Disorders: What Do We Know?" *Harvard Review of Psychiatry* 12, no. 6 (2004): 339–50.

Chapter 5: Facilitator Guidelines

1. R. H. Moos and B. S. Moos, "Paths of Entry into Alcoholics Anonymous: Consequences for Participation and Remission," *Alcoholism: Clinical and Experimental Research* 29, no. 10 (2005): 1858–68.

Chapter 6: Core Topic 1: Assessment

1. K. Humphreys, L. A. Kaskutas, and C. Weisner, "The Alcoholics Anonymous Affiliation Scale: Development, Reliability, and Norms for Diverse Treated and Untreated Populations," *Alcoholism: Clinical and Experimental Research* 22, no. 5 (1998): 974–78. Online issue available May 30, 2006.

2. J. Witbrodt, Y. Ye, J. Bond, F. Chi, C. Weisner, and J. Mertens, "Alcohol and Drug Treatment Involvement, 12-Step Attendance and Abstinence: 9-Year Cross-Lagged Analysis of Adults in an Integrated Health Plan," *Journal of Substance Abuse Treatment* 46, no. 4 (2014): 412–19; L. A. Kaskutas, L. Ammon, K. Delucchi, R. Room, J. Bond, and C. Weisner, "Alcoholics Anonymous Careers: Patterns of AA Involvement Five Years after Treatment Entry," *Alcoholism: Clinical and Experimental Research* 29, no. 11 (2005): 1983–90.

3. L. A. Kaskutas, L. Ammon, K. Delucchi, R. Room, J. Bond, and C. Weisner, "Alcoholics Anonymous Careers: Patterns of AA Involvement Five Years after Treatment Entry," *Alcoholism: Clinical and Experimental Research* 29, no. 11 (2005): 1983–90.

Chapter 7: Core Topic 2: Acceptance

1. *Narcotics Anonymous,* 6th ed. (Van Nuys, CA: Narcotics Anonymous World Services, 2008), 17.
2. *Alcoholics Anonymous,* 4th ed. (New York: Alcoholics Anonymous World Services, 2001), 30.
3. *Narcotics Anonymous,* 6th ed. (Van Nuys, CA: Narcotics Anonymous World Services, 2008), 8.
4. *Alcoholics Anonymous 2014 Membership Survey,* www.aa.org/assets/en_US/p-48 _membershipsurvey.pdf.

Chapter 8: Core Topic 3: Surrender

1. *Narcotics Anonymous,* 6th ed. (Van Nuys, CA: Narcotics Anonymous World Services, 2008), 17.
2. *Alcoholics Anonymous,* 4th ed. (New York: Alcoholics Anonymous World Services, 2001), 25.
3. *Twelve Steps and Twelve Traditions* (New York: Alcoholics Anonymous World Services, 1981), 27.
4. Ibid., 26.
5. *Alcoholics Anonymous,* 4th ed. (New York: Alcoholics Anonymous World Services, 2001), 45.
6. *The A.A. Member—Medications and Other Drugs* (New York: Alcoholics Anonymous World Services, 2011), 4, 6.
7. *Alcoholics Anonymous,* 4th ed. (New York: Alcoholics Anonymous World Services, 2001), 133.
8. *In Times of Illness* (Van Nuys, CA: Narcotics Anonymous World Services, 2010), 20.

Chapter 9: Core Topic 4: Getting Active in Twelve Step Fellowships

1. *Living Sober* (New York: Alcoholics Anonymous World Services, 1998), 13.
2. A. Ellis and R. Harper, *A Guide to Rational Living* (New York: Wilshire, 1975); A. Ellis, *Reason and Emotion in Psychotherapy* (New York: Citadel, 1994).
3. *Alcoholics Anonymous 2014 Membership Survey,* www.aa.org/assets/en_US/p-48 _membershipsurvey.pdf.
4. R. H. Moos and B. S. Moos, "Paths of Entry into Alcoholics Anonymous: Consequences for Participation and Remission," *Alcoholism: Clinical and Experimental Research* 29, no. 10 (2005): 1858–68.
5. L. A. Kaskutas, L. Ammon, K. Delucchi, R. Room, J. Bond, and C. Weisner, "Alcoholics Anonymous Careers: Patterns of AA Involvement Five Years after Treatment Entry," *Alcoholism: Clinical and Experimental Research* 29, no. 11 (2005): 1983–90.
6. J. Witbrodt, Y. Ye, J. Bond, F. Chi, C. Weisner, and J. Mertens, "Alcohol and Drug Treatment Involvement, 12-Step Attendance and Abstinence: 9-Year Cross-Lagged Analysis of Adults in an Integrated Health Plan," *Journal of Substance Abuse Treatment* 46, no. 4 (2014): 412–19.

7. R. Longabaugh, P. W. Wirtz, A. Zweben, and R. L. Stout, "Network Support for Drinking, Alcoholics Anonymous, and Long-Term Matching Effects," *Addiction* 93, no. 9 (1998): 1313–33; J. Wu and K. Witkiewitz, "Network Support for Drinking: An Application of Multiple Groups Growth Mixture Modeling to Examine Client-Treatment Matching," *Journal of Studies on Alcohol and Drugs* 69 (2008): 21–29.

8. J. S. Tonigan and S. L. Rice, "Is It Beneficial to Have an Alcoholics Anonymous Sponsor?" *Psychology of Addictive Behaviors* 24, no. 3 (2010): 397–403.

9. J. Witbrodt, L. Kaskutas, J. Bond, and K. Delucchi, "Does Sponsorship Improve Outcomes Above Alcoholics Anonymous Attendance? A Latent Class Growth Curve Analysis," *Addiction* 107, no. 2 (2012): 301–11.

Chapter 11: Elective Topic 2: Enabling

1. Al-Anon Family Group Headquarters, *Al-Anon Faces Alcoholism,* 2nd ed. (Virginia Beach, VA: Al-Anon Family Group Headquarters, 1984), 182.

2. Carolyn W., *Detaching with Love* (Center City, MN: Hazelden Publishing, 1984).

Chapter 12: Elective Topic 3: People, Places, and Routines

1. E. Kurtz, *AA: The Story* (New York: HarperCollins, 1988).

2. *Living Sober* (New York: Alcoholics Anonymous World Services, 1998), 19.

Chapter 13: Elective Topic 4: Emotions

1. National Council on Alcoholism and Drug Dependence, "Alcohol, Drug Dependence and Seniors," retrieved October 28, 2016, from https://www.ncadd.org/about -addiction/seniors/alcohol-drug-dependence-and-seniors.

Chapter 14: Elective Topic 5: Spirituality

1. S. Carroll, "Spirituality and Purpose in Life in Alcoholism Recovery," *Journal of Studies on Alcoholism* 54 (1993): 297–301.

2. J. F. Kelly, R. L. Stout, M. Magill, J. S. Tonigan, and M. E. Pagano, "Spirituality in Recovery: A Lagged Mediational Analysis of Alcoholics Anonymous' Principal Theoretical Mechanism of Behavior Change," *Alcoholism: Clinical and Experimental Research* 35, no. 3 (2011): 454–63.

3. National Center for Complementary and Integrative Health, "Meditation: In Depth," retrieved October 31, 2016, from https://nccih.nih.gov/health/meditation /overview.htm.

Chapter 16: Introduction to TSF-COD

1. I. L. Petrakis, G. Gonzalez, R. Rosenheck, and J. H. Krystal, "Comorbidity of Alcoholism and Psychiatric Disorders," National Institute on Alcohol Abuse and Alcoholism, November 2002, http://pubs.niaaa.nih.gov/publications/arh26-2/81-89.htm.

2. G. Fein, "Lifetime and Current Mood and Anxiety Disorders in Short-Term and Long-Term Abstinent Alcoholics," *Alcoholism: Clinical and Experimental Research* 37, no. 11 (2013): 1930–38.

3. L. C. Jordan, W. S. Davidson, S. E. Herman, and B. J. BootsMiller, "Involvement in 12-Step Programs among Persons with Dual Diagnoses," *Psychiatric Services* 53 (2002): 894–96.

4. E. Kurtz, *AA: The Story* (New York: HarperCollins, 1988); S. Cheever, *My Name Is Bill* (New York: Washington Square Press, 2005).

5. *The Dual Disorders Recovery Book* (Center City, MN: Hazelden Publishing, 1993), 63.

6. S. Glassner-Edwards, S. R. Tate, J. R. McQuaid, K. Cummins, E. Granholm, and S. A. Brown, "Mechanisms of Action in Integrated Cognitive-Behavioral Treatment versus Twelve-Step Facilitation for Substance-Dependent Adults with Comorbid Major Depression," *Journal of Studies on Alcohol and Drugs* 68 (2007): 663–72.

7. J. F. Kelly, R. L. Stout, M. Magill, J. S. Tonigan, and M. E. Pagano, "Mechanisms of Behavior Change in Alcoholics Anonymous: Does Alcoholics Anonymous Lead to Better Alcohol Use Outcomes by Reducing Depression Symptoms?" *Addiction* 105 (2010): 626–36.

8. E. Triffleman, "Gender Differences in a Controlled Pilot Study of Psychosocial Treatments in Substance Dependent Patients with Post-traumatic Stress Disorder: Design Considerations and Outcomes," *Alcoholism Treatment Quarterly* 18, no. 3 (2000): 113–26.

Chapter 17: Important Considerations for TSF-COD

1. *The Dual Disorders Recovery Book* (Center City, MN: Hazelden Publishing, 1993), 91.

Chapter 18: TSF-COD Treatment Guidelines

1. K. Humphreys, L. A. Kaskutas, and C. Weisner, "The Alcoholics Anonymous Affiliation Scale: Development, Reliability, and Norms for Diverse Treated and Untreated Populations," *Alcoholism: Clinical and Experimental Research* 22, no. 5 (1998): 974–78. Online version available May 30, 2006.

2. J. Witbrodt, Y. Ye, J. Bond, F. Chi, C. Weisner, and J. Mertens, "Alcohol and Drug Treatment Involvement: 12-Step Attendance and Abstinence: 9-Year Cross-Lagged Analysis of Adults in an Integrated Health Plan," *Journal of Substance Abuse Treatment* 46, no. 4 (2014): 412–19; L. A. Kaskutas, L. Ammon, K. Delucchi, R. Room, J. Bond, and C. Weisner, "Alcoholics Anonymous Careers: Patterns of AA Involvement Five Years after Treatment Entry," *Alcoholism: Clinical and Experimental Research* 29, no. 11 (2005): 1983–90.

Chapter 20: Conjoint Topic 2: Caring Detachment

1. M. Beattie, *Codependent No More* (Center City, MN: Hazelden Publishing, 1992), 61.

2. J. Knowlton and R. Chaitin, *Detachment and Enabling* (Center City, MN: Hazelden Publishing, 1985), 6.

Index

Page numbers followed by (f) *indicate figures; page numbers followed by* (t) *indicate tables.*

About the Authors

Joseph Nowinski, PhD, has held positions as assistant professor of psychiatry at the University of California, San Francisco; associate adjunct professor of psychology at the University of Connecticut; and supervising psychologist of the Correctional Health Care division, University of Connecticut Health Center. In addition to *Twelve Step Facilitation Handbook,* Dr. Nowinski is the author of *Substance Abuse in Adolescents and Young Adults: A Guide to Treatment, Family Recovery and Substance Abuse,* and *If You Work It, It Works! The Science Behind 12 Step Recovery* (published by Hazelden Publishing). For additional information visit www.josephnowinski.com.

Stuart Baker worked as a primary clinical supervisor for Twelve Step Facilitation therapists in Project MATCH at Yale University and is licensed and certified as a drug and alcohol counselor in private practice.

About Hazelden Publishing

As part of the Hazelden Betty Ford Foundation, Hazelden Publishing offers both cutting-edge educational resources and inspirational books. Our print and digital works help guide individuals in treatment and recovery, and their loved ones. Professionals who work to prevent and treat addiction also turn to Hazelden Publishing for evidence-based curricula, digital content solutions, and videos for use in schools, treatment programs, correctional programs, and electronic health records systems. We also offer training for implementation of our curricula.

Through published and digital works, Hazelden Publishing extends the reach of healing and hope to individuals, families, and communities affected by addiction and related issues.

For more information about Hazelden publications,
please call **800-328-9000**
or visit us online at **hazelden.org/bookstore**.

Alcoholics Anonymous

Order No. 2021—Alcoholics Anonymous Big Book 4th Edition Hardcover

Order No. 2053—Alcoholics Anonymous Big Book 4th Edition Softcover

Order No. 205320—Alcoholics Anonymous Big Book 4th Edition
Case Special Softcover (1 case of 20 books)

Order No. 202120—Alcoholics Anonymous Big Book 4th Edition
Case Special Hardcover (1 case of 20 books)

Order No. 5093—Twenty-Four Hours a Day Softcover (meditation book)

Order No. 1455—12 Step Pamphlet Collection

Narcotics Anonymous

Order No. 4843—Narcotics Anonymous 6th Edition Softcover

Order No. 4842—Narcotics Anonymous 6th Edition Hardcover

Order No. 7493—It Works: How and Why Softcover

Order No. 4722—It Works: How and Why Hardcover

Order No. 4138—Living Clean Softcover

Order No. 4139—Living Clean Hardcover

Video Resources

Order No. 7593—Discover the 12 Steps Video and CD-ROM

Order No. 7592—Young Adults Discover the 12 Steps Video and
CD-ROM

To order, visit hazelden.org/bookstore or call 800-328-9000.